Sweet SUCCESS

Knowledge and Quick-Skills in Thirty Minutes

CLEMSON BARRY, PhD.

authorHOUSE®

AuthorHouse™ LLC
1663 Liberty Drive
Bloomington, IN 47403
www.authorhouse.com
Phone: 1-800-839-8640

Published by AuthorHouse 02/17/2014

ISBN: 978-1-4918-6243-8 (sc)
ISBN: 978-1-4918-6242-1 (e)

Library of Congress Control Number: 2014902407

SOCIAL MEDIA RESPONSES

After the manuscript was completed, several business owners from my network on LinkedIn were selected, and each person was sent a different chapter to read and critique. With their permission to share their responses, here is what some of them have said:

- "Lots of information and good advice for anybody starting a business." **Ray, California**
- "Refreshing and to the point! You are doing what I am trying to do as well—give some guidance that is positive yet filled with common sense. **Marty Zwilling, founder and CEO, Startup Professional Inc., and author of the book *Do You Have What It Takes to Be an Entrepreneur?***
- "We would love to feature you in our magazine. Please contact editors@ilenecarol.com, and http://issuu.com/. **Ilene Carol, New York**
- "I revisited my financial plan, and I applied the information as you have recommended. I saved $6,558." **Janice, New York**
- "Thanks! I am preparing to expand my business overseas, and I have more confidence now than I had before. I am excited." **Jim. K, UK**
- "I am impressed with the whole chapter and the job interviewing process. I have interviewed many applicants during my career." **Rosie. G, Canada**
- Very good points! Every business owner should revisit those fundamentals on a regular basis." **A. Ridley, Australia**
- "It exceeds my expectation. I plan to use the questionnaires as blueprints to transform my business." **L. Ludgero, Brazil**
- "Interesting, practical, and precise." **K. Adeyeri, Nigeria**

CLIENTS

"Respect doesn't come from the kind of work you do; it comes from the way you do the work."—Kenneth L. Shipley

Everybody cannot do the same job because talents and aspirations vary. If everybody does the same job, economic growth will be stagnated and many of us would not be alive. Hence, vibrant economic activities and economic growth can only come from a diverse labor force that is comprised of people in different trades and professions.

My firm or company, Barry's Accounting Services Corporation is a household name to many clients in the USA and overseas. I focus on the strategic aspects of building a business. Customers' experience (customer service and customer satisfaction) is a priority.

My firm or company serves clients in the following industries:

- **Music and fashion**
- **Restaurant and bakery**
- **Bar and lounge, and nightclub**
- **Beauty and barber shops**
- **Sports and films/movies**
- **Trucking, buses, and limousines**
- **Aviation related**
- **Merchant marine**
- **Shipping and courier/delivery**
- **Medical and service professionals**
- **Real estate and construction**
- **Electrical and mechanical**
- **Hardware and furniture**
- **Manufacturing, wholesale, and retail**
- **Motel**
- **Technology and Internet cafe**

If you would like details of the services I provide for my current clientele, please visit my website: **www.ConsultantBarry.com**

ARTICLES

Here are some of the articles that I have published in professional journals:

- "Managing Business Liquidity"
- "SMEs and NGOs in a Renewed Global Economy"
- "Doing Business Overseas"
- "The Economics of Entertainment and Tourism"
- "Essentials of Inventory Management"
- "Controlling Fraud in Project Management"
- "Mistakes Start-Ups Make"
- "Cross-Selling: An Overlooked Asset"
- "Getting a Record Deal"
- "Outsourcing: A New Economy"
- "Real Estate: Ask the Expert"
- "Growing a Business in a Slow-Growth Economy"
- "Strategies for Entering Markets Dominated by Entrenched Competitors and Big-Name Contenders"

BULK PURCHASE FORM

BULK PURCHASE DISCOUNT and FREE SPEAKING ENGAGEMENT is available if one hundred or more of this book is purchased by individuals, schools, civic groups, associations, and organizations that want to hold practical business workshop for their students, clients, and members. Also, send me a copy of your tax-exempt certificate.

If you are a teacher in Europe, and you are involved with training SMEs, you can use this book in conjunction with the "Erasmus for Young Entrepreneurs" program recommended by the European Union Commission. Fill out this page, tear it out, and e-mail it to me. My e-mail address is: ClemBarry@aol.com

Your name _____

Organization _____

Tax-exempt number_____ Fax_____

Address _____

Your telephone # _____ E-mail _____

Website address _____

Number of books required_____ Date required_____

Payment online: Check and major credit card.
Go to our website, www.Consultant.Barry.com

Number of books shipped_____ Date shipped_____

Carrier_____ Retail price $_____ Your Price $_____

Shipping $_____ Sales tax (VAT) $_____ Total $_____

Your signature_____ Date_____
(Authorized persons only)

A copy of this page will be enclosed as a packing slip with you order.

SPEAKING ENGAGEMENTS REQUEST FORM

(Seminars, conferences, workshops, and opening ceremonies)

Speaker's name: Clemson (Clem) Barry

If your organization needs a speaker, please fill out this form and send it to us. If your offer is accepted, we will contact you. A contract will ensure and a confirmation of your booking will be sent to you when payment is received. You may contact us at Tel # (718) 677- 4006; **e-mail: ClemBarry@aol.com**; **website: www.ConsultantBarry.com**

Check the box: [ ] Seminar only   [ ] Conference only   [ ] Workshop only
[ ] Seminar, VIP meeting, and autograph
[ ] Opening ceremony and autograph

Your Name (Event Organizer) _____
Organization Name_____ **Tel#**_____
Fax #_____ **Tax-exempt Number**_____
Date of event_____ **Type of event (indoor/outdoor)** _____
Venue capacity_____ **Number of attendees** _____ **Unit price $** _____

Event location (full address)_____
Tel#_____ **Police Precinct #**_____ **Your permit#**_____
Name of security company_____ **Tel #**_____

Appearance(s): Dates_____ **Topic:**_____
_____
Duration of time: From _____am/pm   to   _____am/pm.
Amount you are offering:$_____. **Payment is due four weeks prior to the event date.**

Names of other speakers, if any, who will speak at the event
Name _____Topic _____Time _____
Name _____Topic _____Time _____

Other information that you would like us to consider:_____
_____

Sign here_____ **Date**_____
(Decision maker/event organizer)

COACHING REQUEST FORM

"Setting achievable goals and developing action plans"

Coach name: Dr. Clemson (Clem) Barry

Tel # (718) 677-4006; e-mail: ClemBarry@aol.com;
website: www.ConsultantBarry.com

Check one box:　[ ] **One-day accelerated coaching**

　　　　　　　　[ ] **Two-day accelerated coaching**

　　　　　　　　[ ] **Coaching every month for four months**

Your Name _____ Cell # _____

Best time to call _____ E-mail _____

Business Name _____ Tel # _____

What industry are you interested in?_____

What progress, success, or breakthrough have you had in this industry?

_____

_____

What have you avoided, come up against, or struggling to resolve?

_____

_____

What do you expect to achieve at the end of the session?

_____

_____

How soon do you plan to start the session? _____

PLEASE NOTE: Sessions will be customized to meet your needs, and you will receive a training manual. At the end of the session you will receive unlimited support and objective feedback at no extra cost to you.

Published by: AuthorHouse Publishing, USA
Edited by:
Reviewed by:

CONTENTS

ACKNOWLEDGMENTS

This book is an extended and updated version of articles that I have written in professional journals and speeches I have given. I thank the folks at the American Society of IRS Problem Solvers, who gave me my first break—putting me in the "**hot seat**" to speak in front of over four hundred enrolled agents, CPAs, and attorneys at their annual convention, at the Embassy Suites Hotel, Denver, Colorado, in 2005. Speaking and answering questions from the toughest groups of professionals is an opportunity about which some people could only dream.

Special thanks to my clients, entrepreneurs, and many other people who were eager to share their stories with me and encouraged me to write this book. Thanks to all entrepreneurs—past and present—whose mistakes I have learned from and whose success stories inspired me to start my business in 1982 and write this book today.

Special thanks to the thousands of clients that have patronized me and the audiences that have listened to me for over thirty years. I thank the numerous coaches, career counselors, publications, radio stations, and television for helping me launch and develop my career, and everyone who has participated in my private coach/mentor programs.

INTRODUCTION

My name is Clemson (Clem) Barry. I am a taxation and business consultant, coach, author, and speaker. Thanks for buying and reading my book. I hope it will challenge and motivate you to achieve your goals as it has challenged and motivated me to write it. **I also add a *bonus* chapter for you, "Doing Business Overseas."**

This book is an extended and updated version of articles that I have written in professional journals and speeches I have given. I have written this book because I am happy to share my knowledge with people and because many people from various industries, cultures, and countries were eager to share their stories with me and encouraged me to write this book. **My mission is to give you insights into the fascinating world of entrepreneurship and take you step by step from vision to reality**—to challenge you and keep you inspired, to help you see the opportunities in every challenge and motivate you as you continue to build your career, grow your business, and fulfill the vision and dream that you are passionate about, and to help you make a name for yourself.

This book contains a proven step-by-step blueprint that would help you become successful. The best part about this book is you can read a chapter and apply what you have learned in thirty minutes. I am proud to have developed and used those strategies and techniques to start and grow my company, mentor new business owners, and restructure my clients' companies.

You can buy my book, or you can read the thirty-four books that I have listed in the resources section of my book.

If you applied the practical information in this book in a timely and sensible manner, and you genuinely did not get results, **I will be happy to coach you over the phone for *free*, for thirty minutes**. I care too much about my readers and business clients to leave them hanging. Please let me know how you are doing. Send me your comments. My e-mail address is **ClemBarry@aol.com.**   **Thanks for buying my book.**

CHAPTER 1
MONEY TALKS

The "Money Talks" chapter is great. I applied the information as you have recommended, and I am happy to say I saved $6,558.—**Janice, New York**

Our lives are consumed with daily financial transactions in the form of income, savings, investments, and expenses. **A person is earning money, saving money, investing money, or withdrawing money to pay expenses.**

I am sure you have heard the proverbial sayings:

"Money makes the world go around."
"A penny saved is a penny earned."
"Money talks."
"Cash is king."
"Out of money, out of business."
"No money, no honey."
"Money pulls the strings."
"Money in the bank gives a peace of mind."
"A vision without money is just an illusion."
"It is not how much money you make. It is how much you get to keep."

Overview

Anybody who does not believe those proverbs are true should try surviving in this world without having access to money. Financial experts have said almost 90 percent of all marriages that ended in divorce had failed, in part, because of financial problems, financial disputes, or financial disagreements. This is one of the reasons why financial planners encourage a client to pay attention to how a fiancé or fiancée spends money and ensure the client is comfortable with those spending habits before finally deciding to get married. That is also one of the reasons why family attorneys (divorce attorneys) encourage their clients to have lengthy financial discussions with their dates or engaged persons during courtship and have prenuptial agreements drawn up and signed before marriage.

"When you change your thinking, you change your life."

I have worked with thousands of low-, middle-, and high-income clients for over thirty years. Many of them do not pay attention to how they spend their money or accumulate debts. Many of them can't track how much they pay for automobile insurance, fuel, parking, maintenance, and tolls; and they do not have a written budget for other monthly expenses such as mortgage/rent, utilities, student loans, and homeowner's insurance or renter's insurance.

Nothing Ventured, Nothing Gained

I am always surprised at how people who have handled their responsibilities on their jobs proficiently and efficiently are so lackadaisical and disorganized when it comes to organizing and managing their personal finances. Everybody needs a job, and every worker has to perform excellently in order to keep the job, but please remember that the job belongs to the employer, and your finances belong to you. Your finances are what you will get to keep when your employer terminates your service. If you do not have money set aside in **an emergency fund,** then you will suffer severe financial hardship if the company that you are working for today files for bankruptcy next week. Your severance pay and pension would be tied up in bankruptcy court for a year or two, and a monthly check for unemployment compensation may not be sufficient to pay your bills. If you have a mortgage on your home, or if you rent an apartment, the bank and the landlord would not wait for one or two years to get paid. We have seen what happened to many of our friends, neighbors, and family members during the **world financial crisis (economic recession)** that started in 2006. Many of them did not pay attention to how they were managing their incomes and **ostentatious spending**. They were not prepared to weather the financial crisis, so when they lost their jobs they also lost their vehicles and homes or apartments. They have suffered financial hardships because they did not have an emergency fund or savings for a rainy day—money saved to pay expenses for twelve to twenty-four months.

Budget and Credit Counseling

What everybody needs is a simple, thoughtful, and disciplined approach to every facet of their financial lives.

1. **Cash advance and bank overdraft.** You are experiencing financial difficulties if you are required to take cash advances from your credit card to meet your daily, weekly, or monthly financial needs, or if you are required to use your bank overdraft protection to cover checks that you have written. Those are red flags; and they are screaming at you to manage your finances more prudently.

2. **Maybe you are underpaid, and that's why you are taking cash advances.** Research and study the job market to get a feel of your value for the job you are doing. Do salary research on **salary.com** and **payscale.com**. Maybe you would have to take a second job or use your hobby to earn extra money. Make a list of the ways you can earn extra money and get started. (Read the **"Microenterprise"** chapter.)

3. **Finances that are in disarray reflect people who are high risks.** People who fall into that category seldom pay their bills on time because they seldom open their mail and review their monthly statements. They frequently get overcharged, miss deadlines, and pay late-payment charges. Lenders and investors respect low-risk and visionary borrowers who have organized their personal finances before approaching them.

4. **Prepare and stick to a budget that fits your lifestyle and goals**. Be patient; take the time to organize and plan your income and expenses. Set your priorities and monitor and eliminate unnecessary expenses. Look for expenses in your budget that you can reduce, and put the savings into your emergency fund or rainy day savings account. **Note: (On the next page, I prepared two worksheets to help you analyze your finances. Take a look at them right now.)**

5. **Set up an emergency fund or rainy day savings account** to pay sudden and unforeseen expenses. Start saving money today to pay your expenses for twelve months in case you lose your job or get sick. It does not matter if you put $5 per week into this account. When an emergency hits, you will be glad you have money available to pay your bills. **Cash advances** on credit cards, which have high interest rates, and **payday loans** and **car title loans** (using your car title to secure 16 percent of the car value as a loan) are very expensive ways to borrow money.

6. **Have an investment portfolio** to help you build wealth and provide retirement income to cover all your essential and lifestyle expenses.

7. **Sell poor-performing investments, pay off your debts, and take a tax break.** If you have poor-performing stocks and bonds in your investment portfolio, sell them before their value drops lower and use the cash to pay off your debts. You can also take up to $3,000 in tax deductions on your tax return every year if your stocks were sold at a loss.

8. You may also choose to use the extra money to reduce your debts and increase your FICO score by **paying off those debts that have the highest interest rates first**. As soon as one debt is paid off, take that payment and apply it to the next debt.

9. **Transfer your credit card balances to a new credit card, and cut your total debt by 50 percent or eliminate your debt altogether.** Shop around and get a new credit card that offers an introductory rate of 0 percent to 3 percent for the next twelve to eighteen months with no balance transfer fee.

   a. If you have more than one credit card, start by transferring the amount from your credit card that has the highest interest rate to this new credit card. For example, if you transfer $10,000 that you are paying 12 percent interest on, and you continue to pay the same monthly payment on time, you can reduce that $10,000 debt by $5,000 in twelve to eighteen months. You can eliminate your debts altogether in twelve to eighteen months by making bigger monthly payments because most of your monthly payment will be applied toward the principal.

   b. If you have a car loan from your bank or credit union, and **you pay off your car loan** by transferring the balance of the loan to a credit card with a lower interest rate, you

      1) will save on interest payment;
      2) will get title or ownership to your vehicle quickly;
      3) will stop paying credit insurance on the car loan (that alone will be equal to 5 percent or more of your total annual car insurance premium);
      4) can keep liability insurance coverage and cancel collision and comprehensive coverage and save another 55 percent or more of your annual insurance premium. **For example,** if you live in New York and have a clean driving record and a car loan, depending on the kind of car you buy, full insurance coverage (liability, collision, and comprehensive) can cost you $5,000. Liability coverage alone is $2,000. Therefore, when you pay off the car loan by

transferring it to your credit card, and you cancel collision and comprehensive insurance coverage, you will save $3,000 every year. This strategy is perfectly legal, and it can be applied in any state.

10. **Education.** Think long term and stay focused. Make sure what you are studying is what you intend to do as a career. You have to earn money to pay back student loans that you have borrowed, plus income you have lost during the years you were studying in school. If you can't pay your student loan, call your creditor early and ask for a **deferment**—a temporary suspension of your monthly payment for a few months.

11. **Buying a house.** The requirements for getting you qualified to obtain a mortgage will vary. However, the lower your FICO, or credit score, the higher the interest rate and your month payment will be.

    a. You are qualified for a **bank mortgage** if your FICO score is 700, your down payment is 20 percent, and your monthly expenses are less than 30 percent of your monthly income. If you do, you will get the best interest rate from the bank.

    b. You are qualified for an **FHA mortgage** if your FICO score is 560, your down payment is 3.5 percent, and your monthly expenses are less than 30 percent of your monthly income. Having a low credit score means you are not trustworthy with debt. Hence, you will need to increase your FICO score or get a cosigner. **Contact HopeNow.com or HomeFreeUsa.org, and talk with a counselor.**

12. **Home ownership**. If you own a house with a mortgage, and you can't pay your mortgage, call your mortgage company and ask for **forbearance**—a temporary suspension of your monthly payment for a few months. Ask your lender for a mortgage or **loan modification** if the amount you owe for your house is more than the market value of your house. **Contact HopeNow.com or HomeFreeUsa.org, and talk with a counselor.**

13. **Get into a debt management program**. If your debts are uncontrollable, then get into a debt management program and stop debt collectors from calling and harassing you. This program is designed to help deadbeats pay off their credit card balances over a period of time and improve their FICO score with the credit bureaus. The program is operated by nonprofit organizations in your city, county, district, or province, and it is funded or sponsored by the credit card companies. **Avoid getting into a debt settlement program.** If you get into this program, some of your debts

will be forgiven as part of the settlement. However, the total amount that was forgiven is considered income, and you must declare it on your federal and state tax returns and pay income taxes on it.

14. **"A cosigner is just as liable as a borrower."** When you cosign on a loan for a borrower, that loan would appear as an outstanding debt on your credit report, and it will reduce your eligibility to qualify for other loans. The borrower is a high risk, and the lender could not ascertain that the loan will be repaid by him or her. Therefore, you must be prepared to repay the loan if the borrower stops making payments (defaults on the loan). If you refuse to repay the loan, the lender can sue you, and the court's judgment against you will become a lien against your possessions, and they can be sold to satisfy the debt. You may also be required to pay legal fees that the lender incurred to pursue the case against you. That can hurt your FICO scores and future employment position, as employers would evaluate your credibility and question your judgment. Some people would proclaim that the borrower and the lender had conspired against you because you did not benefit from the loan. Although it appears to be a conspiracy, it is legal for the lender to file a lawsuit and get judgment against you.

Problems that some people have encountered

1. **Lack of financial knowledge and the unwillingness to seek and pay for competent advice.** (It is okay to seek financial advice, especially if you want to invest a large portion of your income. However, don't put all your eggs in one basket. Here is an example of how you may design your investment portfolio: cash, CD, and money market 20 percent; real estate 30 percent; stock 25 percent, bonds 25 percent).You can adjust the percentage of each investment to suit your present and future needs.
2. **Lack of an emergency fund or rainy day savings in their budget.**
3. **Poor or bad investment decision—the results of bad timing or putting too much money in investments that cannot be liquidated quickly.**
4. **Spending money irresponsibly (ostentatious spending).**
5. **Victims of inexperience or of predatory advisors.**

*** I have prepared two worksheets for you. The worksheets are shown on the next two pages. You may fill them out manually, or you may use the format to design a similar worksheet on your software program.

Your personal budget or cash flow plan

INCOME	WEEKLY	BIWEEKLY	MONTHLY
Forms W2	$	$	$
Self-employment			
Hobby			
Interest/dividends			
Bonus			
Commission			
Pension			
Social Security			
Inheritance			
Winnings			
Alimony			
Child support			
TOTAL INCOME	$	$	$

EXPENSES	WEEKLY	BIWEEKLY	MONTHLY
Rent/mortgage	$	$	$
Utilities			
Repairs			
Child support			
Alimony			
Helper and gardening			
Loans			
Gasoline/travel			
Food			
Pet care			
Clothing			
Laundry			
Education			
Recreation			
Dues			
Vacation			
Donations/gifts			
Payroll taxes			
Doctor/dentist/pharmacy			
TOTAL EXPENSES	$	$	$
CASH FLOW (NET)	$	$	$

Your Personal Net Worth Plan

ASSETS

Cash—checking accounts $

Cash—savings accounts

Off-shore accounts

Certificates of deposit

Stocks

Bonds

Mutual funds

Notes and contracts

Life insurance (cash surrender value)

Personal property (vehicles, jewelry, paintings,

    Golf clubs, trophy, planes, boats, furniture) $

Pension (IRA, 401K, 403b, SEP, KEOGH, NIS, NIC)

Real estate owned (appraised value)

Other (specify)

Other (specify)

TOTAL ASSETS $

LIABILITIES

Credit and charge cards (balance) $

Notes payable balance (automobiles, etc.)

Taxes payable (Income, Property, etc.)

Property mortgages (balance)

Student loans (balance)

Cosigner on loans (balance)

Other liabilities (balance)

TOTAL LIABILITIES $

** NET WORTH (assets minus liabilities) $

My company and I can help you manage your personal finances if you are too busy to handle them or if financial planning and management is something you don't like doing yourself. Please fill out the request form below and call us.

Request for Personal Financial

Planning and Management Service

Tel # (718) 677–4006; e-mail: ClemBarry@aol.com,
Website: www.ConsultantBarry.com

Financial Planner: Clemson (Clem) Barry
Training: Dunn and Bradstreet (credit and financial analysis)

The College for Financial Planning (personal financial planning, tax planning, retirement planning, insurance planning, and estate planning)

I would like your company to help me manage my financial affairs.

Check one box: [ ] I am too busy to handle my finances.
[ ] It's not something I like doing myself.

Your Name _____ **Cell #** _____

Best time to call _____ **E-mail** _____

What do you plan to accomplish?
_____
_____

How quickly do you want to see results? _____

"It is not how much money you make. It is how much money you get to keep. **Everybody,** including the rich and famous, is concerned about **disposable income.**"

CHAPTER 2
BEAT THE IRS

Overview of UK and USA payroll and consumption tax

In the UK and countries that adapt the European system of taxation, employers or business owners must deduct payroll taxes from their employees' wages. In addition they are subject to collect **value added tax (VAT)** for selling products and services. **In the UK and countries using the European method of taxation, the PAYE system is used to make payroll deductions:**

1. Income tax
2. National Insurance Scheme (NIS/NIC)
3. National Housing Scheme (NHS)
4. National Education Scheme/Fund (NES/NEF)

**In the UK, payroll taxes are reported immediately.

In the USA, employers or business owners must deduct payroll taxes from their employees' wages. In addition, they are subject to collect **sales tax** for selling products and services. Some services are exempt from sales tax.

The USA uses the PAYE system to make payroll deductions:

1. Federal and state income taxes
2. Social Security and Medicare taxes
3. Unemployment and workers' compensation tax

** In the USA, payroll taxes are reported quarterly.

Taxation in the USA

I am sure you are familiar with the proverbs:

"It is not how much money you make. It is how much money you get to keep."

"Collecting more taxes than is absolutely necessary is legalized robbery." *—Calvin Coolidge*

"Make sure you pay your taxes; otherwise, you can get in a lot of trouble." *—Richard M. Nixon*

"The hardest thing in the world to understand is the income tax." *—Albert Einstein*

"The taxpayer: that's someone who works for the federal government, but doesn't have to take a civil service examination." *—Ronald Reagan*

"The difference between death and taxes is death doesn't get worse every time Congress meets." *—Will Rogers*

The IRS wants people to pay more taxes. We want to make sure that those clients who hire us would not experience undue hardship while paying the IRS. I work with clients every day to keep them out of trouble with the IRS, and I work with IRS's auditors every week to settle tax cases. I know their procedures and how to get my clients' case in front of an auditor who would make a favorable decision. I let the auditors know in advance that my clients have to pay living expenses and put food on the table, and unfavorable resolutions will provide a hardship case for them.

My areas of expertise:

1. Allegation of dubious expenses
2. Allegation of underreporting income
3. Allegation of misclassification of workers
4. Business Income and expense reconstruction
5. Doubt about tax liability

6. Allegation of tax fraud
7. Liens, levies, and seizures
8. Settling payroll, sales, and income tax debts
9. Like-kind exchange and installment sales
10. Interest and penalty abatement

Tax planning, preparation, and business and financial management consultations throughout the year, with a focus on debt management for clients in the following industries: entertainment, construction, retail, transportation, real estate, and medical. **www.ConsultantBarry.com**

Overview

Under what circumstances will a person receive a letter from the taxing authorities?

A taxpayer will receive a letter from the taxing authorities if:

1. The taxpayer has failed to file tax returns.
2. The taxpayer's tax return(s) was audited.
3. The taxpayer is delinquent in paying taxes.

Why should a person file a tax return?

Everybody should file their tax return every year to avoid paying penalties for failure to file and also to take advantage of the statute of limitation, which expires three years after you file an accurate tax return. The taxing authorities have forever to come after taxpayers who did not voluntarily file their tax returns.

Who should file a tax return?

According to US income tax laws, every US citizen and permanent resident living in the USA or overseas must file their income tax returns every year, whether or not they have had income during the year.

What kinds of income are we talking about?

People must report their worldwide income, including income that they have earned offshore. It does not matter whether the income was obtained legally or illegally. Income earned by a US citizen or a permanent resident living overseas, and by sailors sailing in international waters is considered US income regardless of where the sailor lives. However, they may qualify for the Foreign Earned Income Exclusion and the foreign tax credits for taxes paid to a foreign country. Wages, salary, or professional fees paid to a foreign worker while working in the United States of America is considered US income, even if the employer is a foreign corporation, and payments were deposited into a foreign bank account.

"The U.S. taxes all income wherever you earn it. So forget arguing that only foreign-source income is taxable, making your domestic income exempt. There is a convoluted argument that foreign income is different, but don't bother with that argument. In fact, a variation of this bogus theory is the one that got Mr. Wesley Snipes in trouble and consigned to three years in prison." —*Forbes Magazine, August 12, 2012.*

"The argument that filing and paying income tax is unconstitutional has failed. I don't think any defendant in a criminal tax case (or in a civil tax case for that matter) would be well advised to rely on this argument. Taxpayers should be wary of any such arguments or of promoters touting these theories." —*Robert Wood, tax attorney, WoodLLp.com*

How much income tax is enough?

Income tax can be defined as the amount of money that governments take from our wages or salaries. Our income tax system is a pay as you earn system. Hence, the amount of income taxes that we are obligated to pay varies from time to time as our incomes change and governments change the tax rules and tax rates to collect more tax revenue. Hence, the more money we earn, the more income taxes we are obligated to pay.

How could a person pay less tax?

In the United States of America, taxpayers who want to cut their tax bill can:

1. Use tax planning methods to legally reduce their income taxes. Amid the complexity and uncertainty of today's economy, more and more taxpayers are turning to tax planning. This is called tax avoidance (not tax evasion), and it is perfectly legal.
2. If you have worthless stocks in your investment portfolio that you can sell at a loss, sell them and get up to $3,000 in tax deductions every year.
3. Take the itemized deduction. Itemized deductions are taken by one out of four taxpayers to reduce their tax bill further. Taxpayers can add up their deductible expenses and take the itemized deduction if that deduction is higher than the standard deduction. The catch is that the government can ask those taxpayers to present documentation to substantiate or justify their claim.
4. File amended tax returns if all the tax deductions people were entitled to were not taken on their original tax returns. Your claim may be legitimate; however, it will open your original tax return to scrutiny, so be prepared to defend your original tax return and your amended tax return. One way you can avoid an audit of your tax returns is to file your amended tax return two weeks before the end of the statute of limitation for the original tax return.

Why are receipts and records important?

You may forget to report some of your income and expenses if you did not record them when they occurred. Also, you are required to keep records in case government auditors ask you to substantiate tax deductions that you have taken on your tax return. If you cannot produce the required documents to support your claim, and if you cannot give plausible and valid reasons why you cannot defend the deduction and credits on your tax return, then your deductions will be classified as **dubious deductions**, and the auditor will charge you additional tax, interest, and penalties. The auditor may also want to charge you for **tax evasion**. Tax evasion is a criminal tax offense that has landed some taxpayers in prison.

Tax loopholes

Taking a tax deduction that was authorized by the government is not a loophole. We can argue about the merit of some deductions, but they are certainly not loopholes. Tax loopholes denote that the tax laws were stretched beyond their intended purpose. This is an old trick that some tax shelter promoters used to sell **tax shelters** to investors. They promised investors big tax breaks and huge tax savings. The IRS would get suspicious and audit those tax shelters and either disallow some or all of the tax deductions; or allow the investors to take tax deductions that are equal to the actual cash amount that they have invested in the deal. Either way, investors are usually hit with a huge tax bill.

Private letter ruling

The IRS issues free private letter rulings to taxpayers who ask for them. You should obtain your own private letter ruling in advance if you have decided to invest in a tax shelter or similar investments in the United States of America or offshore. A private letter ruling that was issued to one taxpayer does provide valuable insights about the IRS's position. However, another taxpayer should not rely on it even when the factual situation is similar or identical. You should ask for a private letter ruling:

1. When a tax shelter promoter promises you big tax deductions and huge tax savings
2. When the tax law is not clear, or when you cannot find a positive tax case or court decision to support your belief or decision
3. When the tax laws require that taxpayers obtain private letter rulings in matters that pertain to tax shelters, tax-free transactions that involve foreign corporations, and offshore investments

Gray areas

A gray area in tax law is an area where no clear legislation or precedent exists, or where the law has not been applied in a long time, thus making it unclear if it is applicable at all. Disagreements may occur during the interpretation of tax laws over factual matters. It is usually about whether a particular tax law should be interpreted as the IRS suggests. The dispute or issue can be settled at the Appeals Division of the IRS, the Public Advocate's Office, or the federal tax court.

How can a person survive an income tax audit?

If you are audited, you can represent yourself, or you can hire a tax professional to represent you at the audit. If you choose to represent yourself, you must meet with the government tax auditor and present to him or her the records that you have used to prepare your tax return. If your records are accurate, then they should be sufficient to substantiate the deductions that you have taken on your tax return. If during the audit you disagree with the auditor's findings, don't be disrespectful to the auditor, and don't try to bribe him or her. The honorable thing to do is to tell the auditor that you would like to suspend the audit and hire a tax professional to represent you. That is your right, and it is perfectly legal to ask for a suspension of the audit.

If you have adequate records, but meeting with a government tax auditor does not make you feel comfortable, or if you have taken **dubious deductions** that you did not have adequate records to substantiate, then you should hire a tax professional who has in-depth knowledge of your profession or in-depth knowledge of your industry to craft your presentation or construct, reconstruct, and prepare your tax return correctly and present it to the government auditor. [Taxpayer rights to consultation and representation, Sections 7521 and 7811; restriction on examination of taxpayer, Section 7605(b); IRS publication 1, treasury regs. 26CFR601.105 and 26CFR601.106(b), internal revenue manual, IRM 4043.1(2), IRM 4015(1), and circular 230].

"My tax problem is over, and I am feeling better now. For four years, I've felt like I was on the lam." —*Jayson S, Brooklyn, New York*

What can you do if you owe tax after an audit?

You can do one of the following:

1. You can choose to pay the full tax bill immediately and then file a claim for refund (Forms 843 and 911) for abatement of interest and penalty if they were assessed erroneously and illegally against you (Section 6404).
2. You can choose to sign an installment agreement (Form 433-D) and pay you tax monthly. However, if you fail or refuse to honor your obligation, the IRS would freeze your bank accounts and/or put a lien on your property **(lien, levy, and seizure).**

What can you do if you owe tax, and you can't pay?

If you owe income taxes for several years, you can request that the government consolidate those taxes and send you one tax bill. You can then sign an installment agreement and pay the bill monthly. However, in order to maintain your installment agreement, the government will require that you file your future tax returns on time. Failure to do so will render the agreement null and void.

If you no longer have the ability to pay because of terminal illness, or your income has deteriorated to a point whereby you can honestly declare financial hardship (Form 911), then you should prepare and file with the government a **"Statement of Financial Condition," or Form 433**; and request to settle your tax under one of the following:

1. **"Collateral Agreement," Form 2261** (Give assets to satisfy your debt. Singer Dionne Warwick had that agreement with the state of California several years ago.)
2. **"Offer-in-compromise," Form 656** (Settle for pennies on the dollar.)

Business tax

Employers' responsibilities:

1. **Request withholding information from all employees—Form W4.** (Failure of an employer to comply and collect payroll taxes is a felony under Section 7202.)
2. **Deposit payroll taxes they have collected.** (An employer who refuses to send payroll taxes to the government because the money was used to pay suppliers and operating expenses will be charged, in addition to the tax owed, a penalty that is equal to 100 percent of the amount of the payroll tax that should have been withheld and sent to the government. The 100 percent penalty [**trust fund penalty**] is recompense to the government for breach of fiduciary trust by the business owner—Section 6672.)
3. **Prepare and file all payroll tax returns** (including forms W2 and W3, and furnish forms W2 statements to employees—Section 7203 and 7204).
4. **File the business tax returns** (File the year-end tax returns and business and payroll records and have them available upon request by the taxing authorities—section 6001.)

Tax audit

Tax auditors are aware that people would do almost anything to avoid paying taxes. There were occasions when the information on business returns appeared to be accurate, when in fact those tax returns were filled with inaccuracies. Another fact is that governments would not hire thousands of tax auditors if they trusted taxpayers.

1. Transparency

If a tax auditor feels your business deductions are inconsistent or are higher than those in your industry, then a red flag goes up. If your business is audited, the burden of proof will rest on you, so be prepared to defend yourself and your **business.**

2. Skimming from the top

Underreporting business income. That is, reporting less income than the business had earned.

3. Dubious deductions

   a. Overreporting business expenses. That means inflating items of expenses that are relevant and recognized in your business and the **industry.**
   b. Deducting expenses that are not appropriate or recognized in your **industry.**

4. What should business owners do?

Avoid comingling of funds. Open a business checking account and a personal checking account.

   a. Deposit business income and pay business expenses from the business checking account.
   b. Use your business account and business credit cards to keep track of your business expenses.
   c. Avoid paying personal expenses from your business accounts. This strategy will prevent the auditor from prying through your personal accounts and poking his/ her nose in your personal affairs.

d. Everything that you purchased in your name should be paid from your personal accounts. Keep your personal income and pay your personal expenses from your personal checking, savings, and credit card accounts. For example:

1. Payment that you made for building materials that you purchased to maintain your private home should be paid from your personal accounts and not from your business accounts.
2. Monthly payments that you made for an automobile that you purchased or leased in your name should be paid from your personal accounts, even if part of the payment you made can be classified as a business travel deduction.

What should everybody know about owing back taxes?

1. They will not disappear if you continue to ignore them.
2. They will continue to accumulate compound interests and penalties.
3. They will affect a delinquent taxpayer's credit score.
4. They can be levied against a taxpayer's property and paychecks.
5. Some taxes cannot be discharged in bankruptcy.
6. People have been sent to prison for refusing to pay taxes.

You can be sent to prison for dodging the taxman if you continue to ignore written correspondence sent to you or your accountant. There are famous actors, singers, and sports figures that have had to honor bench warrants and had to postpone their tours/shows and return to their country or states to settle their tax disputes. If you apply for a mortgage, the banks will insist that you file and pay all back taxes before you can close on a property. Sure, you can buy it in someone else's name, but he or she can sell the property and pocket the proceeds, and there is no legal recourse. If you own a business, access to funding at low interest rates is critical for growth and success of your business, but tax liens can hurt your chances of obtaining loans from banks and credit from suppliers.

I appreciate feedback from my readers and clients. My e-mail address is **ClemBarry@aol.com**, and my website is **www.ConsultantBarry.com**.

CHAPTER 3
CUSTOMER SERVICE

I am sure you are familiar with the following proverbs:

"Nobody cares about how much you know until they know how much you care."

"It is nice to be important, but it is important to be nice."

"Relationship is the key."

Overview

There was a time when customer service used to be the reason why customers would choose one store over another store and one company over another company. Today, companies are so focus on generating profits and living up to the expectations of shareholders and the stock markets that customer service has become secondary to low prices (price wars). Managers know low prices are the only things that will bring bargain hunters and price-conscious customers into their stores. To meet their sales target, customer service is relegated to lip service, empty promises, and toll free numbers to register complaints with offshore telemarketing centers to make customers feel their companies really care.

Your company's ability to provide customers with good customer service and exceptional value or benefit for their money is the reason they will choose to give you repeat business and send you referrals, which are the lifeblood of your company. Customer service is about getting customers to see the importance or value of what your company is offering and what they are buying. You should pay close attention to customers' activities, get feedback from them, and acknowledge their points of view because customers' feedback would be your biggest ally. It would give you a competitive advantage in the marketplace.

Employees come first

"The task ahead of me is never as great as the power behind me."
—Ralph Waldo Emerson

In the real world of business, employees should come first. They represent the company, and they are the ambassadors and advocates for the company. If you treat them like business associates, train them properly, and reward and support them fairly, they would elevate your brand, create value for your company, and convert customers into ardent supporters and strong advocates for your products and services. Take a look at companies such as Starbucks, Costco, and hotels that are owned and managed by Marriott.

"There is only one boss, the customer; and he can fire everybody in the company from the chairman on down, simply by spending his money somewhere else". — Sam Walton

That is a good way to train and coach employees. However, that philosophy can also be a mind-controlling technique to discourage employees from asking for pay raises and fringe benefits, because customers would shop elsewhere if prices are increased. Meanwhile, the founders, their heirs, and their executives are earning millions of dollars in dividends from annual profits, while those hard-working employees are earning a pittance.

Sure, businesses need customers, and customers are in control of the customer-business relationship. However, customers also need businesses to provide services for them that they cannot or would not provide for themselves. Therefore, customers should be courteous to the people who are serving them; or they should take their business elsewhere. If you operate a high-quality and transparent business, and you are catering to the right consumers, then you should be able to get new customers to do business with you.

Customers are not always right

Company supervisors must be able to manage the dual challenge of customer-employee relationships. When customers become intolerable or unbearable, managers should exercise their authority and demonstrate courage and practical brilliance and refer those customers to competitors. It is time to tell them, **in a very subtle way, to *"get lost"*** or ***"take a hike."*** I have done that many times as a manager and as a business owner.

It is not right for customers to shoplift. Shoplifting is a criminal offense. **I have listened to judges and IRS auditors telling feisty lawbreakers that they can't always have it their way. There are feisty customers who will always want to have things their way. However, companies have rules by which workers and customers must abide.** If your company keeps bending backward to appease every customer, unscrupulous customers would take those courtesies as weaknesses and abuse those privileges and your employees. I have seen customers assault employees in order to boost their fragile egos when their unreasonable demands were rebuffed.

People who work in customer services and reservations departments usually complain that they felt humiliated and betrayed when their supervisors knew they acted right but did not back them in disputes with customers who were making unreasonable requests and demands and were not speaking truthfully in their complaints. Those employees said they felt their supervisors did not handle those disputes tactfully, and within their company's guidelines, and they have lost confidence in the culture of those companies.

Settling customer disputes or misunderstandings

I have learned from experience that a dispute has three components or elements:

1. The customer story
2. The employee story
3. The truth

Settling issues or complaints against employees does not mean employees were acting inappropriately or rude toward customers. It means opening the lines of communication to include customers' complaints, employees' defenses, company policy, availability of services or products at the time of disputes, prices at the time of the disputes, alternative choices customers could have made, ethics, and moral and legal principles that must be applied to reach an amicable settlement.

Responses from supervisors whom I have contacted:

1. "It is a tough job, and I settle disputes the best way I could."
2. "Our customers know the rules when they make reservations, and when they check in at the front desk they get a booklet that reminds them about the rules— service, respect, integrity, and honesty."
3. "Sometimes it is easier to side with customers and get them off my back."
4. We operate at a certain standard, and we value the safety of our workers. If customers' requests are unreasonable, I will tell them my company cannot meet their demands, and I will refer them to a competitor."

The truth shall set you free

"Have the courage to say no and the courage to tell the truth. Do the right thing because it is right. Those are the keys to living your life with integrity." —W. Clement Stone

Don't promise customers the world and then turn around and tell them you cannot fulfill your promise. Unscrupulous behavior is counterproductive to the integrity and culture of your brand.

Customers like to know they are getting a bargain. They are delighted when they receive a little more than they paid for. However, every so often companies would advertise and promise the world to get customers to do business with them. If your company makes outrageous promises to get customers to patronize it, and those promises were not fulfilled to customers' expectations, then your employees in customer services or reservations will feel the wrath from customers' hostile reactions.

I have realized that if you commanded their respect from the beginning, you will have few or no issues with them. It is better to tell customers the truth upfront and let them take their business elsewhere if they choose to do so, than to lie to them and get them angry. With the advent of the Internet and social media, angry customers can become dangerous customers.

Your competitive edge

Competitors are not buying your products and services, so don't waste your time thinking about them. Give only 2 percent of your attention to the competition in order to keep up with changes in the marketplace and in your industry.

Customers are buying your products and services so focus on your customers, and give 98 percent of your attention to customer feedback and customer service, and learn everything that you can about your customers, including but not limited to: customers' needs, wants, preferences, buying patterns, income, wealth, birthday, anniversary, etc.

In a competitive industry, customer service is sometimes the only thing that differentiates one company from another, and it cannot be easily imitated or copied. The best example is the unique service that you give to your customers. It is important to respond to customers in a timely manner and with insightful information. How you answer questions, settle disputes, respond to compliments, and correct mistakes or errors can make or break your relationship with customers and their community of friends on social media.

Competitors may speculate about the kind of service that you will provide to a typical customer. However, competitors are not mind readers, and they cannot determine the level of service you will provide to each of your customers on a particular day, since business owners will usually go above and beyond their service policy to accommodate customers. Apart from having a monopoly in the marketplace, high-quality service would definitely distinguish your business from your competitors, hence the reasons why high-price brands such as Mercedes Benz, BMW, Rolex, etc., are flourishing.

They focus on the needs of their customers and the complaints and feedback they received from their customers to improve their customers' experience. They are customer focused, and they are honest with their customers. They say what they would do, and they do what they promised. They have had good experiences with those brands, and those brands have given them value for their money and peace of mind.

Customer service survey

A survey that was done for a well-known retail store has quoted 71 percent of consumers saying that their biggest turnoff is sales personnel who are not helpful, knowledgeable, and friendly. While quality of merchandise or service should be a priority at your establishment, whether online or off, it is interesting how much importance was placed on service in a physical store. Yet when customers walked through the aisles of many large stores that could afford to hire workers, they could hardly find a worker there to help them.

Customers feel abandoned, and they retaliate by stealing millions of dollars in merchandise. Hence, shoplifting has become the norm, and stores are responding by installing cameras instead of hiring workers to patronize customers or security personnel to patrol the aisles.

We are aware that dealing with the public is the toughest job that anybody can have, so we asked some experienced customer service representatives in the hospitality, retail, and travel industries to comment on their most recent experience with customers. Here is what they have said:

1. Rude.
2. Impatient.
3. Demanding.
4. Inconsiderate.
5. They want something for nothing.
6. They watch their TVs, and they see how well superstars are being treated. They come into the store, hotel, or airline office and want to be treated like superstars, and they can't pay for the preferential treatment.
7. They want to speak to the boss and nobody else, even when someone else is available to help them.
8. Somebody got them angry, and instead of leaving their problems outside the door, they come in here with their anger and want to treat us like dirt. We are not their dumping ground.

How others are coping

In order to keep a good relationship with customers, especially those that are difficult to deal with, some professionals such as accountants and contractors often bypass an argument with a client or customer and calm the client or customer by asking this question:

Which part of the project or assignment do you want to pay for, and which part do you prefer to do for yourself?

After the client has answered the question, the next step is the valuation process to see if the client is a good or right fit for the firm or company:

1. The value of the service that has to be provided
2. The ability of the client to pay
3. The future potential/value of the client
4. Efficiency with which the client handled the engagement (cooperation, temperament, etc.)

I appreciate feedback from my readers and clients. My e-mail address is **ClemBarry@ aol.com**, and my website is **www.ConsultantBarry.com**.

CHAPTER 4
HIRING EMPLOYEES

"I don't care if it is a white cat or black cat as long as it can catch mice." —Miyamoto Musashi

I am sure you have heard these proverbial sayings:

1. **"Great employees build great companies."**
2. **"You are as good as the people you hire and train."**
3. **"If you are searching for well-cut diamonds, you may never find diamonds in the rough."**

Who is an employee?

According to the US Internal Revenue Service (IRS) rules, an employee is anybody who performs services for an employer if the employer has control over what must be done and how the work will be done. This is so even when the employer gives the employee freedom of action. What is important to remember is that the employer has the right to control the details of how the work is to be done or how the service is performed and the benefits that the worker received or the benefits that were paid on behalf of the worker.

Regulations and enforcement

In many countries, including the United States of America, Canada, and the United Kingdom, the taxing authorities are aggressively pursuing companies that have misclassified their employees as independent contractors in order to avoid paying their share of the employment taxes (tax evasion).

Under section 3402 of the US Tax Code, all employers are required to deduct and withhold federal income tax from their employees' wages and remit those income taxes to the federal taxing authority (IRS).

Employers who are caught breaking this rule will face the following charges:

1. Penalty for "failure to pay"—0.5 percent of the total unpaid tax under (Tax Code section 6651). This penalty is applied to every month, or part of the month, for withholding taxes that are due and remained unpaid.
2. Penalty for "failure to file" wage reports—5 percent of the due and unpaid tax (Tax Code section 6651). This penalty will be applied every month (or partial month) until all wage reports are filed.
3. Criminal fines, arrests, and imprisonment (Tax Code §7203). A conviction will lead to a fine, up to $25,000 (or $100,000 for a corporation). That fine can be substituted for, or combined with, imprisonment for up to one year. There's also a 75 percent penalty associated with many convictions.

Job-searching essentials

There was a time when people would attend one interview and get hired. People were interviewed and hired by their immediate bosses or supervisors, such as plant managers, foremen, office managers, warehouse supervisors, chief accountants, etc. Applicants had strong work ethics, and the process was simple. Applicants had to know what the job entailed and prove they knew how to accomplish the work. I was hired every time I attended an interview. Nowadays employers want every applicant to have a credit check and a background check, and they are also snooping into your Facebook, Manta, LinkedIn, and Twitter accounts.

I have worked for companies that operate in fifteen industries. I have been through a lot of job interviews as an employee and as a business consultant. I would like to take you through the modern interviewing process. Here is the "inside scoop."

Job search or job hunting is tough work. Today a job search can be compared to starting and grow a business. You have to be patient, focused, optimistic, passionate, and resilient; and you will be required to invest a considerable amount of time cultivating or building a strong network of referrals, including friends, recruiters, headhunters, and employees who are working for your potential employers.

1. You must identify potential employers whom you believe would be interested in using your service and whom you believe would share an interest in your career goals and development. It is about what you can do for your potential employer and what your potential employer can do for you. That is the first thing that your potential employer would want to discuss with you in a very supple and psychological way to carefully evaluate whether you would be the right fit for the company and whether the job you want would be a positive and progressive step for you. They know you could lose interest in the job and become a drain on your team and start looking for another job three to six months after they spend a lot of time and money training you.

2. Do your due diligence or research about potential employers. Know their history and understand their business operations and business culture. Recruiters and potential employers are thrilled about hiring people who are fully prepared and ready to make money for them.

3. Research the salary that the job pays to know what you are worth. You can do salary research on **salary.com** and **payscale.com**.

4. Market yourself effectively by preparing resumes that target each potential employer. Also, each cover letter that is attached to each resume should state specifically what job or position you want and how your potential employer would benefit from your knowledge or expertise. Demonstrate how you plan to cut costs, reduce expenses, improve productivity, increase market share, or increase revenue. Every job or new position has a learning curve, and employers are thrilled about people who are capable of learning quickly and producing results quickly. Please let me know about your success.

Recruitment sources

Employers can recruit potential employees who have sent in their resumes to the company, and sometimes employers may use other sources to recruit new workers, such as:

1. Referrals from trusted employees
2. Recruiting on school campuses
3. ecruiting from school placement assistance officers
4. Employment agencies
5. Headhunters

How employers select applicants

I have contacted five employers and I asked each employer this question: What do you look for in an applicant before you would consider hiring the applicant? Each employer gave me a different answer. Their answers are written randomly. Here is the response from each employer:

1. A person who is responsible, has good communication skills, integrity, and is passionate about learning, developing, and making a career of what he or she is doing.
2. Someone with a proven track record, who understands the task, who is organized, and has the ability to execute and deliver.
3. Anybody who is entrepreneurial, who has a desire to help others, who has strong and proven communications skills, and can solve complex issues.
4. A person who is intelligent, hardworking, and responsible. That person must demonstrate technical skills, soft skills, and leadership ability.
5. A generalist, someone with an aptitude to work on any assignment or work in any department instead of having to confine himself or herself to doing one thing.
6. I always asked applicants where they wanted to be in five years. When they said they wanted my job, or if there is an indication that they want my job, they did not get hired.

"When I interview a job applicant, I am on the lookout for someone whom I believe can work well on a team and lead it, either now or in the future."
—Sander Van't Noordende, group chief executive, Accenture.

What are soft skills?

People who have soft skills are able to communicate well, demonstrate common sense, respect, integrity, empathy, and patience. Those skills together with their technical or hard skills are what employers are looking for in all recruits. People who have a combination of soft and hard skills are poised for leadership positions.

Diversity of employees

Diversity of employees is imperative to contend with globalization and the multicultural business environment that it encourages. Diversity would broaden your company's customer base, increase its market share and value; and stabilizes its income or revenue.

Employees' expectations

"Give us credit."

In some companies, people who work in customer services or reservations departments usually complain that they felt humiliated and betrayed when their managers or supervisors knew they were right but did not support them in disputes or disagreements with customers. They said they felt their managers or supervisors did not handle disputes tactfully and with integrity, and they had lost confidence in their company's culture.

"We are human beings."

Every worker expects good working conditions. In October 2012, there was a massive and violent strike at the Lonmin's Platinum Mine in Marikina, near Rustenburg, in South Africa. The miners complained that the mine owners had received funding from one of the international lending organizations with a stipulation attached to develop the local community. They claimed the owners had reneged on the stipulation in the contract, and they had abdicated their responsibilities, and that had caused them to be living in deplorable conditions, in rented tin shacks surrounding the mines, and there continued to be prolonged problems with their wages, housing, health, unemployment, and the environment. They felt they were marginalized, and their only alternative was to fight for social justice and human dignity.

"Pay us what we are worth."

Every worker expects to earn a living wage. Many companies, including Nike and Ikea, had to issue formal apologies and make reparations to victims who were paid low wages (forced labor) to make products that sold at high prices and high margins worldwide. Some of those companies have said their contractors and subcontractors were to be blamed for this atrocity. That excuse did not appease public anger because in the court of public opinion, there are no statutes of limitations and no forgiveness if a business has committed an immoral act against the less fortunate people in society.

KFC, Pizza Hut outlet shut indefinitely
Republica, August 15, 2012
Devyani International currently employs 180 people in Nepal. On Tuesday the company announced an indefinite closure of KFC, Pizza Hut, and Cream Bell outlets, citing labor problems.

"We are forced to shut down our services for an indefinite period of time, under existing labor laws, after workers at our franchises manhandled the chief of the HR Department. Some staff members have refused to take instructions from management. They have beaten their managers and threatened to take their lives. The franchises will not be opened until the company fires all workers who are currently working for KFC and hires new workers. Workers will not get paid during the time the franchises were closed.

However, the president of the All Nepal Hotel and Restaurant Workers Union-Revolutionary (ANHRWU-R) refuted the charges. In a statement he said, "We are not involved in those activities as claimed by the franchise management. We have decided to form a workers union, and management decided to close the outlets by issuing a notice. A team of 66 staff members had applied for registration of our union at the labor office on August 07, 2012, when the company's HR manager tried to stop the registration process. Members of the union had proposed to hold talks with management, but they refused to hold dialogue.

Virtual employee

Under the US tax code, an employee who has received permission to work from home instead of commuting to work daily and who must check in regularly with his or her employer via telephone, e=mail, or conference call, and who is required to attend company meetings at least once a week or once monthly, may qualify for the office-at-home deductions.

Preparing for a job interview

Every prospective and hired worker must share the company's values, and he or she must be the right fit for the company, otherwise the company will be wasting valuable resources to train and motivate the person. After your resumes and application forms are reviewed by your interviewer, the following would happen:

1. You will be introduced to the group or team members with whom you will be working if you are hired, and you will be answering questions from them. This meeting is a good chance for you to shine and for the recruiter to get feedback from team members about your soft and hard skills.
2. You will be introduced to various executives in the company who would hold a steady conversation with you. This meeting is a good chance for you to shine. You will be interacting with them, and they will be asking you questions that pertain to your background, goals, career paths, and knowledge of the industry. They would be listening to your answers and carefully observing your demeanor and body language.

"I had employment offers from five companies. In my rounds of interviews with each company, I met consistently brilliant, professional, passionate managers and partners. I knew I wanted to be like them someday, and the decision was clear which company I would choose." —Olivia Chiu, analytics consultant at Accenture

Interview Questionnaire

1. Why do you want to work for this company?

    _____

    _____

2. How long will it take for you to make a significant contribution to the company? Why?

    _____

    _____

    _____

3. You have met and spoken with people who will be part of **your group**. What do you
    hope to achieve from **working in this group?**

    _____

    _____

4. How do you plan to establish your credibility quickly **with the team?**

    _____

    _____

    _____

5. How would your position fit in with the career path that you envisioned for yourself?

    _____

    _____

    _____

6. How do you envision yourself working in this industry in the next ten years? (That
    should be an intellectual conversation about the state and direction of the industry,
    and applicants should not be afraid to agree or disagree and support their decisions
    with solid facts.)

    _____

    _____

    _____

7. Tell me about a manager for whom you had worked and why you had liked or disliked him or her.

_____

_____

_____

8. Discuss a project that you had worked on and the research you had done.

_____

_____

_____

_____

_____

9. Discuss a time when you went above and beyond expectations to offer excellent customer service.

_____

_____

_____

10. Describe a situation where you and a coworker didn't get along. What was the issue? How was the issue or dispute resolved?

_____

_____

_____

11. Discuss a time when you had worked on a team and encountered a problem. What was the problem? How did you resolve the problem? What was the final outcome or result?

_____

_____

_____

_____

** **Please pay special attention to questions #3 (your group) and #4 (the team).**

** If you apply for a job in the Marketing Department, your group may consist of two or more people in your department. However, your team would consist of everybody in the Marketing, Sales, and Advertising Departments.

** If you apply for a job in the Payroll Department, your group may consist of two or more people in your department. However, your team would consist of everybody in the Payroll, Human Resource, and Accounting Departments.

** If you apply for a job in the Credit and Collections Department, your group may consist of two or more people in your department. However, your team would consist of everybody in the Credit and Collections, Sales, Delivery, and Accounting Departments.

During the interview you will be graded for:

1. Specifics
2. Vision
3. Emphasis on ethics
4. Debt of knowledge
5. Responsibility
6. Problem-solving skills

The grades you obtain would enable personnel or the recruiter to evaluate your capability.

Employee compensation package

In most countries, employers or business owners must deduct income taxes (payroll taxes) from their employees' wages. **Countries that are using the PAYE system make some of the following payroll deductions:**

1. Income tax
2. National Insurance Scheme (NIS/NIC)
3. National Housing Scheme (NHS)
4. National Education Scheme/Fund (NES/NEF)

In the United States of America, employers must:

1. Deduct federal and state income taxes
2. Deduct and match Social Security and Medicare taxes
3. Pay unemployment and workers' compensation taxes

How do employers reward their employees and motivate them to produce more while they reduce employee retention and maintain operations and payroll costs within budget? Here are four ways:

Salary

Every worker expects to earn a living wage and have benefits and good working conditions. Your employer's job is to ensure those requirements are met while they monitor and control payroll expenses. Employers usually pay close attention to the following:

1. Changes in employment laws with which their company must comply.
2. Wages, salaries, fringe benefits (perks), and working conditions that workers are requesting and their competitors are offering.
3. Increases in the company's portion (employer's portion) of employment taxes. If the total cost of your employer's portion of employment taxes is higher than competitors' costs, chances are your employer will price itself out of the market if it is selling the same product and competing for the same customers or clients.

4. If new employment taxes are imposed, your employer will revisit and revise the administrative budget (payroll expense) and then meet with the sales staff to review the product or service lines and customers' purchasing patterns. Sales staff must set a higher sales target to cover increases in the overhead costs. They would accomplish the task by looking for ways to push the best-selling services or products while the company reduces or eliminates weak services or products. If the sales force fails to reach the sales target, then the company must bring its business expenses in line with its revenue and the expense benchmarks in the industry by taking one or more of the following actions:

    a. Cut waste and abuses of time, perks, expenses, and supplies
    b. Reduce overtime work
    c. Impose a temporary hiring freeze
    d. Impose work furloughs
    e. Hire new full-time workers at lower salaries
    f. Hire more part-time workers
    g. Lay off some employees and outsource work to them as independent contractors

Fringe Benefits

1. Perks

These include the employer portion of Social Security and Medicare taxes paid on your behalf, medical and dental insurance, travel allowances, pension contribution, maternity and paternity leave, business lunches to accommodate your clients, paid vacation and sick days, scholarship fund for your dependents, tuition reimbursement, paid lunch and dinner when you work overtime, limousine to go home when you work at nights, and birthday presents. Some employers may give all the benefits shown above while others may not give much.

2. Training and continuing education

We live in a very competitive and fast-paced world in which everything has a short shelf life. Skills that you may consider excellent today may become obsolete next week.

Hence, you would need to constantly improve your knowledge and skills so that your company will be able to survive in the marketplace. Take advantage of training and continuing education programs that are available from your employer. Also, ambitious employees, suppliers, and customers would not have patience with companies that are too slow to invest in employee training and new technology.

When I was employed with a large corporation, one of the themes that was constantly repeated in weekly staff meetings was the idea that part of a manager's job was to groom the next person in line to take his or her job. If a manager did that effectively, then the next job that is higher up the ladder would be available to him/her.

I can honestly tell you that grooming people who could replace me was a tricky and gut-wrenching proposition, but I survived, and I was able to build my own business while I worked for my employers. I was able to quit those companies without getting fired or being forced to resign. I have friends who have trained people and were fired when their trainees were competent enough to replace them.

3. Leadership development

A company would not be able to survive for decades without the skills and knowledge from new leaders. Hence, every business owner or CEO is charged with developing and preparing the next group or next generation of workers to lead the company. Hence, workshop training should focus on:

a. Improving ethics and integrity
b. Managing and eradicating wastes and abuses of company time and assets
c. Clear, effective, and smooth flow of information throughout the company
d. Innovation, and improvements in marketing and productivity
e. Improvements in managers' effectiveness, employee morale, employee retention, workplace conflicts, and employees' interpersonal relationship

4. Employee Stock Ownership Plan (ESOP)

Your employer's goal is to attract, hire, and retain performance-driven employees. If the business is profitable, your employer would establish this plan as an incentive to boost employees' moral and increase their productivity. Employees will be allowed to buy company stocks and become investors in the company. This plan enables business owners to raise capital from inside the company to acquire other companies and to pay off existing shareholders. Some companies, including Starbucks Corporation, offer their employees this incentive.

Asking for pay increases

1. Union workers

If you are a union worker, your union would negotiate your pay raises when the labor contract comes up for renewal.

2. Nonunion workers

If you are not unionized, then you must negotiate your salary. Some employers give salary increase annually. Some employers don't give raises even when cost of living expenses are rising to the roof. **They don't care about inflation or the increase in gas prices. They want you to earn your pay raises**.

You may want to have you salary reviewed because you are not getting paid what you feel is a reasonable salary for the work you are doing. Here are some of the reasons why you are underpaid:

a. The person who was doing the job before you came onboard earned the same salary or a lower salary and did the full workload without complaining.
b. Your company may have interviewed several applicants, and your salary fell within their salary range. Hence, your company could get people to do your job for the same salary they are paying you.
c. You did not research the job market and ask for a raise.

"Attitude is everything"

You must fight for your raises, but you must also help your boss protect his or her job. Your boss has to answer to a higher authority. Hence, you must do your homework and visualize the result. Therefore, do the following before you approach your boss and ask for a raise:

1. Research and study the job market to get a feel of your value for the job you are doing. You can do salary research on **salary.com** and **payscale.com**.
2. Be prepared to show how much money you have earned for the company, how much money you have saved the company, or everything that you have done that benefited everybody in the company.
3. Talk to recruiters and headhunters and evaluate the feedback you are getting.
4. Be prepared to give up something to get something (option package), such as work on weekends, more flexibility to work from home, work nights (flex times), or travel for the company. Travel for the company is a hectic job. It is not something that everybody wants to do, but it pays handsomely, and your job will be more secure than most people who don't travel for their company.

You have done your homework, and you are satisfied that you should get a raise. Put your documents into a folder and knock on your boss's office door. Enter the office and present your case with confidence.

How or why employees are fired

1. **Insubordination**—disrespect for authority.
2. **Poor work performance**—a failing grade after repeat warning during performance review and evaluation.
3. **Company downsizing**—reducing staff due to economic recession, loss of market share to competitor, or getting out of a particular market completely.
4. **Merger and acquisition**—your company merged with another company, or it was acquired by another company, and there is **duplication of duties**, whereby two or more employees in your department are doing the same job—**job overlap**.
5. **New management**—A new manager or CEO is hired to restructure your department or turn around the company. The present manager or CEO and some or all of the workers will be fired because they are associated with or contributed to the problem. They will be replaced with new people who are loyal to the new manager or CEO.

** Most companies are closed on weekends (Saturdays and Sundays), so employees are usually fired on Fridays. They get two days at home to grieve, recover from the shock, and move on with their lives.

"There are no guarantees ... only opportunities."

I appreciate feedback from my readers and clients. My e-mail address is **ClemBarry@ aol.com**, and my website is **www.ConsultantBarry.com**.

CHAPTER 5
LEADERSHIP

"There is no limit to what a man can do or how far he can go if he doesn't mind who gets the credit."
—Robert Woodruff and President Ronald Reagan

Poor leadership and bad management are the number one reason most businesses fail. Success in business today is dependent on visionary and creative leaders that are knowledgeable about business best practices and how those practices are applied in their industries.

There can only be one leader, and that person is the business owner or the CEO. Managers and employees will be looking to him or her for guidance, empathy, and improvement in the flow of information throughout the company, and suppliers, lenders, investors, and other stakeholders are counting on him or her to demonstrate leadership and be transparent and consistent at all times.

To clearly understand the expression, ask yourself the following questions:

1. Who does everybody in the company work for?
2. Who is in charge of the company?
3. Who will ultimately be held responsible for the actions of managers, supervisors, and employees?
4. Who will be held accountable by stakeholders and the board of directors for mismanagement of the company?

Choosing a CEO

The person in charge must be able to lead by example. She/he should be diversified, hands-on, know the business and the industry thoroughly, and effectively manage all aspects of the company's operations and finances. That person is a team builder, partner, good listener, proactive leader, calculated risk taker, and an honest, competent, flexible, and passionate advocate or cheerleader who can articulate a clear vision for the company and communicate it effectively to the managers and employees, thus enabling a smooth flow of information throughout the company. And she or he will partner with staff members in all departments of the company to execute the business agenda (improving efficiency and building relationships among employees, suppliers, investors, and creditors, and increasing production, sales, and market share while reducing debts and eradicating waste, fraud, and abuses), while thanking them and awarding them for their accomplishments.

A CEO must answer to stakeholders if the company does not meet the numbers as predicted by the financial markets and the board of directors. Leadership is tough, and a leader cannot take a laid-back approach in the execution of his/her duties. A competent leader must be able to make tough and sometimes unpopular decisions in order to discharge his/her duties effectively. Just because a leader gets tough doesn't mean his/her leadership is tarnished.

Corporate culture

The culture of a company is the pattern of behavior, thinking, and belief of the people that are working for the company. It is the shared experiences, stories, beliefs, values, and practices of everybody who works at the company—its executives, managers, and employees.

Upper management sets the tone that sets the value of the company. These trickle down to lower management and employees. The attitude of everybody who works for the company will send a signal to stakeholders about how much the business does or does not care about people or its environment. The tone at the top is always reflected in the attitude of the people that work for the company. Their actions can motivate customers and creditors to do business with the company and can encourage employees to stay with the company, or they can scare customers, creditors, and good employees away.

Here is what an employee has told me: **"I moved to another company that offered me better pay, benefits, and opportunities to grow. As soon as I started the job, I realized the culture there was wrong for me if I wanted to establish a long-term career with this company. I returned to my former employer, where I was treated well and was given opportunities to learn and grow."**

Benefits of a good corporate culture:

1. Improves employees' relationships
2. Improves employees' mood
3. Reduces worker turnover
4. Increases productivity
5. Encourages employee referrals
6. Attracts the best investors, recruiters, and applicants

Team spirit

Team spirit or team effort, effective communication, and feedback are important to build a strong foundation and a successful company. Hence, the chief executive officer (CEO) should install strong communication and behavioral policies, and use compliance oversight to ensure information from employees at the bottom reaches him or her. Many times employees and managers at the bottom feel they are not important to the company because their concerns or requests to upper management for equipment, tools, or supplies are constantly ignored. **They feel neglected by the company, and they become frustrated because there is a disconnect in the lines of communication. That mind-set could hurt productivity and the business culture of the company. Sometimes the CEO is unaware of what is happening, and that could sabotage his or her accomplishments**.

This situation also exists when some departments believe certain information (segregation of duties) should not be shared with other departments. For example, credit and payment information about a customer may not be easily accessible by a dispatcher, and accounts payable information may not easily be accessible to a shipping manager. This can also be a situation when departments are competing for attention and preferential treatment to the detriment of other departments and without regard to the overall goal or benefit of the company.

Although the CEO must delegate responsibilities to managers in various departments and hold them accountable for breach of fiduciary responsibilities, it is imperative that the CEO has an open-door policy and makes it a habit to take regular tours throughout the company and personally:

1. Meet with every employee.
2. Watch their performances.
3. Ask pertinent questions about what should be done to make their job easier and more efficient, and questions about their managers.

The CEO must intervene quickly to break communications barriers and adopt a business culture and a working environment that increase communications, efficiency, and productivity.

Negotiation

A business owner or CEO must possess strong negotiation skills or delegate this job to people who have it. Good negotiations ensure that all parties benefited from the negotiations and the transactions. Strong negotiation skills would strengthen business relationships with employees, customers, suppliers, creditors, and government agencies, as well as grow the network of stakeholders and ensure future business opportunities.

Strategic planning

Strategic planning involves changes in a company's method of operation or changes in the status quo to ensure future survival of the company.

Why should a business owner or CEO involve staff members in the planning process?

1. To get them to move out of their comfort zones of business as usual.
2. To remind them that everybody is important to the company and get them to reveal new ideas, problems, and hidden agendas, and to listen to them debating over the issues. This is more than brainstorming. It is about disagreements, criticisms, openness, emotions, care, concern, beliefs, and solutions that could not have been predicted before the meeting.
3. To get them to contribute to the plan as a team. When people are committed to the developmental and implementation process of the plan, the odds are greater that the plan will become successful.

Sexual harassment in the workplace

This is a human rights issue, and it is also a health, education, and socioeconomic problem. **This is a form of violence in the workplace**. The International Labor Organization (ILO) defines this offense as: **"An often subtle but disturbing form of aggression."**

Sexual harassment is defined as any verbal, physical, or nonverbal conduct of a sexual nature that affects the dignity of every gender. According to figures from the **Unite Nations**, more that 25 percent of women (worldwide) experience unwanted sexual advances, verbal suggestions, physical contact, and other forms of sexual hostility at their jobs. At the time of this research, the figures for sexual harassment against men were not available.

According to people at the **Bureau of Gender Equality**, sexual harassment; verbal, physical, and psychological abuse; and bullying, mobbing, violence, and job-related stress affect every profession, sector, and gender.

Victims are scared to report this crime because they fear they would lose their jobs, and other employers would be afraid to hire them. It is a hidden problem that has tangible (social, financial, and economic) consequences to:

1. Employees

    a. Increased stress and high blood pressure

    b. Increased risk of job-related accidents

    c. Loss of motivation to work

    d. Loss of respect for the company values or business culture

2. Employers

    a. Absenteeism

    b. Increased employee turnover

    c. Lower job performance

    d. Lower productivity

    e. Potential for surprising and violent retaliation by victims; hence, the life of everybody (guilty and innocent) on the job is at risk

    f. Poor risk management—potential for your insurance premiums to double or triple, or for your insurance to be canceled

Eradicate this unnecessary evil and increase your company's productivity, save it thousands of dollars in health and risk-related insurance premiums and millions of dollars in lawsuit settlements, and get a bonus at the end of the year.

Hiring friends and family members

You will be tempted to hire friends and family members because of your close relationship with them and because you want to provide employment opportunities for them. However, don't hire them if you strongly believe you would have to be tolerant and permissive of their inappropriate behavior and poor work ethics, and you would not be able to develop the courage to fire them.

When you own or manage a business, you have to make tough and sometimes unpopular decisions. Hiring family members and friends can be a blessing if you lead by example, and you are able to get them to separate friendship from business and work diligently for your company and for their salary. However, hiring family members and friends will become a curse when you fire them. They would feel you have betrayed them, and other family members and friends would get involved. That could hurt your relationship with everybody.

You can overcome those obstacles if, during the first interview or during orientation, you outline and explain the rules, regulations, guidelines, expectations, and consequences for breaking the rules, and you lead by example by abiding by those rules, and you enforce those rules by reprimanding all employees for not complying with them. If you can't develop the courage to fire workers for demonstrating poor work ethics and inappropriate behavior, then you are a weak and ineffective owner or manager.

Performance evaluation

It is imperative that you have a system that would help you evaluate your employees' monthly, quarterly, or annual performance. Performance evaluations will help you set specific goals and evaluate or assess the performance or accomplishment of each employee. It keeps employees' focus on key objectives and holds them accountable for specific job performance.

Communication

Workers pay attention to the behavior of their leaders. Therefore, company managers and supervisors must at all times demonstrate consistency in what they say and do. If you own a small company, staff meetings should be held regularly, on the first day of every week, and you should encourage openness, suggestions, and feedback; and team members should be rewarded for innovation, making money for the company, and saving the company money. **"Celebrate what you want to see more of." —Tom Peters**

Oftentimes, companies would base their values on teamwork and team spirit, and managers would keep blowing their horns loudly about that and then turn around and reward one member of a team instead of rewarding every member of the team. This action is somewhat hypocritical, and it usually kills the innovative and motivational spirits of other employees because it defeats the true purpose of the company's value system.

Discussions should be centered on the company's value systems, innovation, culture, and strategies. Meetings should bring everybody up to date about certain behavioral patterns of which the company approves or disapproves. The focus should be about work ethics; criteria for credit approval; sales and collections; customer service; customers' complaints and solutions; present markets; inroads you planned to make in new markets; what competitors are doing; new entrants making inroads into your market; care of equipment, plant, tools, and vehicles; waste and abuse of time materials; supplies; etc.

Research has shown that when a member in a peer group asks a question, it stimulates the thinking of other members in the group, and the various answers or responses that ensued have increased the knowledge and understanding and reduced the learning curve of those in the group.

Managing phone bills

If your company provides cell phones to its sales or field employees, then it is imperative that you **make them sign a pledge** to use their phones for company business only. All of your company **phone bills should be audited monthly**, and each **employee should be held accountable** for using the company phone to transact personal business or make personal calls. Abusive use of phone calls will usually occur during the weeks and months when business is slow, and employees are idle. **Try that solution and save your company hundreds or thousands of dollars monthly or annually and get a bonus at the end of the year**.

Managing expense accounts

If your employees have expense accounts or company credit cards that they can use to entertain clients during business encounters, then it is imperative that you **make them sign a pledge** to use their expense account for accommodating company clients only. **Expense accounts should be audited monthly**, and every charge on the account should be compared to the size of the sales or transaction that your employee obtained during the meeting with the customer. Those procedures would minimize or eliminate abusive practices. Try that solution and save your company hundreds or thousands of dollars monthly or annually and get a bonus at the end of the year.

Transparency

After you have selected your employees, you should emphasize team work or team spirit. If your company designs and sells products, then you would be required to hire designers, technicians, and/or engineers. Everybody in your technology department should work in tandem with people in your sales, marketing, and accounting departments to understand how the innovations and products they will create need to be sold—teamwork. Hence, innovation, costs, and selling price must blend nicely into your product to attract buyers. I have seen many beautifully designed products get rejected by retail stores such as Walmart and Costco because the selling price of each product that was rejected was above the price the retailers would buy them in order to make a reasonable profit. Don't lose faith in your products if they are rejected by superstores such as Walmart and Costco. Selling is full of rejections, and your faith in your business and products will constantly be tested. They may not buy your products, but other stores will be happy to take your products on consignment and sell them at a higher margin, so shop around your products and keep an open mind.

Should the HR Department be in charge of payroll processing? Or should one employee be in charge of payroll, bank deposits, and paying the bills because it is cheaper for the company?

From an **internal control** point of view, payroll process is a joint effort between the HR Department and the Accounting Department, of which the Accounting Department is the paymaster. **The HR Department** is required to provide a statement to the Accounting Department that contains the names and identification of existing employees, their attendance records, salaries, increments, promotion, information about new employees, and firing, with supporting documents attached. **The Accounting Department** is responsible for checking HR statements, reconciling the payroll account, processing the payroll and financial statement, and advising the bank about disbursements. In addition, the **Internal Audit Department** will perform payroll reviews at regular intervals as a form of **"checks and balances,"** to maintain efficiency, accuracy, and segregation of duties.

If the HR Department is allowed to process payroll, or if one employee is allowed to process payroll, make bank deposits, and pay the bills of the company, then the possibility of paying **"ghost employees"** and **committing fraud** would be high because there is **no segregation of duties**.

Many employers thought they were saving money by paying one employee a regular salary to process the payroll, make bank deposits, and pay the bills (accounts payable). Those employers were naïve, and over a period of time their employees embezzled thousands of dollars ($20,000 to $500,000) from their bank accounts. Those employees claimed their employers were taking advantage of them by paying them the same salary to do their job and the job of one or more other employees who should be hired and paid to do the extra work. Employers who are paying one employee the same salary to do everything should insure and bond the employee with a surety company. However, surety companies may not accept the risk because it is too high.

Be accessible

A television documentary series is called **Undercover Boss.** Almost everybody who paid close attention to the series came to the conclusion that those in upper and lower management should get up from their chairs in the corner offices, visit the production areas frequently, and get to know their employees and what it takes for them to accomplish their assignments. In fact, people in upper management should take a page from the operations manual of Southwest Airlines and roll up their sleeves and try doing some of the work themselves for one hour that their employees have to do every day.

When you meet with your employees on a regular basis like Sam Walton used to do at **Walmart**, or when you work alongside your employees in various departments for one hour every month like Herbert (Herb) Kelleher use to do at **Southwest Airlines**, or when you meet regularly with your employees such as Jim Sinegal used to do at **Costco**, you become aware of what it takes to get the job done. You understand the contribution workers are making, and they appreciate you and your company because you have shown respect and appreciation for the work that they are doing; hence, the reason why those employees like to work for those companies.

I have seen employee come up to those business owners and hug them, and I have heard them telling their bosses, "This is the best company that I have worked for. Thanks for hiring me." That compliment made me shake my head in disbelief because compliments like that are rare; but you could see the sincerity and literally feel the bond that these employees have with those companies. I was happy to experience the occasion.

When you, the boss, isolate yourself from your employees, they feel that you have abandoned them. Hence, Herbert (Herb) Kelleher, founder of Southwest Airlines; Sam Walton, founder, of Walmart; Jim Sinegal, cofounder of Costco; and founders of other companies who have aligned their business strategies, innovation, and cultural integrity have had a distinct competitive advantage over their competitors.

Telecommuting

The advent and development of modern technology has enabled people to sit in the comfort of their homes and conduct business around the world. Some employers have capitalized on this modern trend, and they have allowed valuable employees who live in different time zones and rural or suburban areas, far away from their workplace, to work from home and commute to work less often, about one or two days per week or month. Working from home is sometimes referred to as telecommuting or working remotely.

This flexible work arrangement has enabled employees to have a "*work-life*" balance by moving out of their cubicles on the job and working in inspirational settings at home. This has increased employees' loyalty, maximized their time and productivity, and saved them and their employers money. Many employees have voted their company as "The best company to work for." However, in 2013 this flexible work arrangement has gotten bad publicity as Yahoo CEO Marissa Mayer has stated her intention to eliminate the practice because she believes the workers have abused the privilege, and Best Buy stores have set strict rules and policies to ensure that employees who are working from home are productive.

One employer in California who has twenty employees, five of whom work remotely, has told me he can use VPN logs on his computer server to track the productivity of those off-site workers. However, as a small company with a staff of tight-knit workers, he does not want to erode the trust that his workers have placed in the company. Hence, with input from his staff, his company has developed an effective tracking system that alerts everybody.

Terminating the employee

Use these guidelines when you decide to fire or terminate the service of an employee:

1. Have the employee's last paycheck and termination documents ready as prescribed by labor laws. The laws may vary from state to state and country to country.
2. Meet with the employee privately and request that a manager is present at the meeting as a witness to corroborate your reasons for terminating the employee. Do not belittle, disparage, or humiliate the employee in front of his or her former coworkers. **This is not a television sitcom or a movie where actors waived their rights and are barred from suing the media company.**
3. Be direct about the legal reasons for terminating the employee. There is no legal basis for terminating an employee just because you do not like him or her. Unlawful termination will bring bad publicity and a lawsuit.
4. Ask for the employee's keys and access cards to the building and automobile if the employee has access to company vehicles.
5. Ask security to collect the employee's belongings and escort the employee out of the building. In some cases security personnel will be required to drop the employee at the nearest bus stop or train station, or at home.

The whistle-blower's act

The SEC Program

Over the past five years, several countries have passed new laws or strengthened existing laws to protect whistle-blowers. In the United States of America, the "Whistleblower Protection Enhancement Act of 2012" is administered by the Securities and Exchange Commission (SEC). It was enacted to encourage, reward, and protect employees at financial institutions for reporting suspicions of wrongdoing or fraud inside their companies after they have reported their concerns to their employers. This was evidence during the accounting and financial scandal that led to the collapse of several major corporations, notably Enron, WorldCom, and Arthur Anderson, after which Congress passed the Sarbanes-Oxley Act in 2002, holding the CEO and CFO accountable and criminally liable for fraudulent financial reporting acts or financial shenanigans at their companies. There were 164 complaints filed under this act.

Passage of the Dodd-Frank Act in 2010 has extended the whistle-blower act to the private sector. This program is also administered by the Securities and Exchange Commission (SEC).Whistle-blowers can collect 15 to 30 percent of any fine that exceeds $1 million that a company must pay as a result of the whistle-blower's original information and voluntary cooperation. Employees who have suffered a backlash from their employers in retaliation for snitching on them can pursue claims against their employers in federal court.

When the law was first enacted in 2012, the SEC reported that a total of 3,001 whistle-blower complaints were filed. This includes 2,507 complaints from workers in the United States of America. The SEC paid out 10 percent of the budgeted $452 million that it had allocated for paying rewards. The SEC does not reward informants who were part of the original fraud. Tips came from all fifty states, the District of Columbia, and Puerto Rico, and from forty-nine foreign countries. Among those foreign countries, the United Kingdom, Canada, and India filed the most complaints. Complaints range from:

1. Corporations' financial disclosure (18 percent)
2. Fraud (15 percent)
3. Financial manipulation (15 percent)

The IRS program

The Internal Revenue Service has a whistle-blowers program similar to the one that is administered by the SEC. However, the IRS will pay whistle-blowers who have participated in the crime. In September 2012, the IRS paid $104 million to a former UBS banker who gave information in which UBS Bank and the former banker helped wealthy clients hide money from the US government. The information has helped the US Treasury collect $780 million in fines from UBS Bank. However, the former employee spent thirty months in prison before receiving the $104 million because it was alleged he had withheld pertinent information from US Treasury investigators.

I appreciate feedback from my readers and clients. My e-mail address is **ClemBarry@ aol.com**, and my website is: **www.ConsultantBarry.com**.

CHAPTER 6
FIFTIES AND JOB HUNTING

"You are never too old to set another goal or dream a new dream."
—Les Brown

"For every failure, there's an alternative course of action. You just have to find it. When you come to a roadblock, take a detour."
—Mary Kay Ash

I am sure you are familiar with the following proverbs:

"Age is just a number."
"Relationship and connection are the keys."
"Experience is a great teacher."

A lot of people have lost their jobs and investments during the worldwide financial crisis that started in 2007. Some of them will have to work beyond retirement age, and many of them may never be able to retire. They:

1. **Lost their retirement savings in the stock market**
2. **Lost their money in real estate investments**
3. **Were victims in Ponzi schemes and lost their life's savings (TV series** *American Greed*)

People over age fifty that have lost their jobs are finding it difficult to get hired. Some recruiters believe getting people over age fifty back to work is akin to overcoming age discrimination.

How could people who are over age fifty convince potential employers to hire them?

1. They must identify potential employers whom they believe would be interested in using their service. It is about being an asset to employers.

2. They must spend time doing research about each potential employer to learn about its history, and they must be knowledgeable about the business operations and the business culture.

3. They should research the salary that the job pays. They can do research on **salary.com** and **payscale.com**.

4. They must market themselves effectively by preparing resumes that target each potential employer. Also, each cover letter that is attached to each resume should state specifically what job or position they want.

5. They must convince potential employers that although they have been unemployed for a long time, they are up to date with what is happening in the industry. They can show proof of seminars, workshops, and trade shows they have recently attended, as well as research they are doing and valuable connections they have made. They must demonstrate clearly how they plan to improve productivity, increase market share, or increase revenue. Those are some of the things that recruiters and potential employers want to discuss to carefully evaluate whether prospective applicants are the right fit for their companies. Potential employers are thrilled about hiring people who are fully prepared and ready to make money for them.

Successful job seekers

"Never, never, never, never give up."
—Sir Winston Churchill

1. Jane Hall, age fifty-six, found a new job at a law firm in Los Angeles, California. She creatively uses her sales skills to look for business opportunities for the firm's clients using the data-analysis techniques that she learned as a sales manager at her former employer.

2. June Moreno, age sixty, was laid off from her job with a gas and oil company in Texas. After being unemployed for several months, she landed a job with

Sphere Offshore Solutions, another Texas-based company. She brought to the new company specialized knowledge and strong connections, which are key strengths for assembling crews quickly, because in her industry a bad hire can mean an ecological disaster. She said she would hire workers in their seventies because they are the people who have the experience upon which her company relies.

3. At age 64, Jim Hendrickson, a former human resources manager, was out of work for four years. He remained positive by taking continuing education to keep his skills sharp, joining professional networking groups, e-mailing and phoning contacts, and starting a page on the social media site LinkedIn. He mailed and e-mailed twelve job applications every week. His networking paid off when a consultant friend told him about a social services agency that was searching for a human resources manager. He gave the consultant his resume and cover letter, and he received an interview with the agency. He was interviewed for one hour by the agency's director of finance and the chief executive officer. Two day later, he was called back for another one-hour interview with the chief executive officer. He was offered the job one week later. Due to a slow economy and financial constraint, the agency paid him less than he earned at his former employer, but he was grateful for the opportunity to return to work.

Research

An article written by Nathaniel Reade for the AARP has stated the following:

1. Researchers at the University of Mannheim, Germany, studied the teams of workers at the BMW factory and found that productivity has increased as workers get older right up to the retirement age of sixty-five. This is because experienced workers know how and where to focus their efforts, and they thoughtfully handle unexpected problems and prevent costly mistakes.
2. A new study from North Carolina State University has concluded that older computer programmers knew a wider variety of topics than younger workers did, and they also answered questions better and were more adept at certain new systems.

Arguments for hiring older workers:

1. Quality of work compensates for slower speed.
2. ttention to detail is also better.
3. Workplace accident rate is lower.
4. More experienced workers are more careful.
5. Older workers are more loyal and reliable.
6. They have a strong network of contacts.
7. hey are detail oriented and organized.
8. They have leadership, listening, writing, and problem-solving skills.

Arguments against hiring older workers:

1. They are more likely to burn out faster.
2. They are resistant to new technology.
3. They will be absent due to illness.
4. They are poor at working with younger supervisors.
5. They are reluctant to travel.
6. They are less creative, less productive, slower mentally, and more expensive to employ than younger or midcareer employees.

Peter Capelli, professor of management studies at the Wharton School of Business in the United States of America has analyzed research in the fields of economics, demography, and psychology, and he has concluded that the arguments against hiring older workers could not be substantiated. **He believes those hiring managers have listed a litany of stereotypes to explain why they would reject older job seekers.** He concluded by saying, **"When it comes to actual job performance, older workers have trashed their younger colleagues. The juxtaposition between the superior performance of older workers and the discrimination against them in the workplace does not make any sense."**

I agree with professor Capelli. I would also add that the arguments against hiring older job seekers and for firing older employees are just excuses that hiring managers and supervisors make up to convince their board of directors and shareholders that they are great at cutting costs when in fact they are intimidated by older and more experienced workers. I have had clients who have successfully

sued companies and hospitals for illegally firing them. Those employers have fired those managers as soon as the lawsuits were settled, and those workers were reinstated in their jobs.

"Life is a game: Be a player or be played."
—Dr. Phil McGraw

In the news

(Courtesy the *Huffington Post*)

Hy Goldman, age 99, Celebrates 72 Years At Same Company. Goldman, who will turn 100 years old in August 2013, has worked at Capitol Lighting in New Jersey for 72 years. He was hired by Ethel Lebersfeld, who founded the company in 1924 along with her husband Max Lebersfeld, an electrical contractor and immigrant from Austria-Hungary. The family-owned organization is now under the direction of a fourth generation of Lebersfeld.

Employer Vita Needle Proudly Hires Older Workers In Their 70s And Beyond. It's an era in which older workers do what they can to hide their age on their resume out of fear of age discrimination. If you're applying to Vita Needle, the Needham, Mass.-based, needle manufacturer, the hiring managers would consider it an asset.

Rosie, the original Riveter is still on the job at age ninety-three.

By Mike Taibbi, Correspondent, NBC News.

LONG BEACH, Calif. — Remember that cliché "Age is just a number?"

Meet Elinor Otto, age 93, who gets up at 4 a.m. every morning and drives to the Boeing plant in Long Beach, California, where she inserts rivets into the wing sections of C-17 cargo planes. This is a job she has been doing at various aircraft assembly plants since 1942.

I appreciate feedback from my readers and clients. My e-mail address is **ClemBarry@ aol.com**, and my website is **www.ConsultantBarry.com**.

CHAPTER 7

INDEPENDENT CONTRACTORS

Government action

In many countries, individuals must meet certain criteria in order to be legally qualified as independent contractors or self-employed individuals. In the European Union, Canada, and the United States of America, government officials are aggressively pursuing companies that have misclassified their employees as independent contractors in order to avoid withholding income taxes from their employees' wages and also to avoid paying the employers' portion of the employment taxes. **This is called tax evasion, and it is a criminal offense in many countries.**

Each case about **"employee v Independent Contractor"** is judged on its own merit. However, if an employee relationship exists, the taxing authorities would classify the independent contractor as an employee.

Safe harbor

My advice to everybody who wants to work as independent contractors and freelancers is as follows:

1. Form a corporation or limited liability company.
2. Open a business checking account and deposit payments and withdraw your salary and business expenses from that account.
3. Have business stationery (business cards, letterhead, contract forms, and invoices).

What is important to remember is that as an independent contractor or freelancer, you are on your own. The employer does not have the right to control the details of how the work is to be done or how the service is to be performed; and you are not entitled to receive any benefits apart from the contract price for your service. Hence, you must price your work or service appropriately.

Ignorance of the law

A company hired workers and classified them as independent contractors. The company paid them their full wages and didn't withhold income taxes from their wages. Three of the workers were laid off after working for more than six months for the company. They could not find work, so they went to the Department of Labor and applied for unemployment compensation. The Department of Labor contacted company officials, and after meeting with them, the department paid those workers and demanded repayment plus a huge fine from the company. The Department of Labor determined that the company had complete control over the workers and the details of how the work was done; and company officials should have properly classified them as employees and withheld income taxes. The department also said the company had willfully chosen to classify those workers as independent contractors (Forms 1099) in order to evade the employment taxes. Company officials' actions were considered willful disregard for employment rules and regulations.

Increase your income

Several years ago, people depended on one source of income. Today, people can leverage their expertise and earn income from several sources **(multiple income streams).**

Many professionals have **income streams** from teaching, speaking, writing, consulting, investigation coaching and training clients, and expert witness.

Some professionals and nonprofessionals earn new **income streams** from working in a second job, such as jobs from hobbies and by moonlighting.

Many artists (singers, musicians, actors/actresses) have **income streams** from several sources, such as:

1. **Appearances** (promotional, opening act, headliners, movies, and fashion)
2. **Tickets and VIP packages** (private parties, concerts, and tours)
3. **Royalties** (record companies, copyright infringement, music publishing, book publishing, radio playlist, songwriting, film and movie soundtracks, etc.)
4. **Ancillary /residual** (studio rents, merchandise sales, endorsements, sponsorships, and advertisers)

Why do companies outsource?

In her book *Ninety Percent of Everything*, **Rose George, a British journalist and author,** states: "It's less expensive to ship Scottish cod 10,000 miles away to China to be filleted and then sent back to Scotland than it is to pay Scottish workers to do the job. Of course, this reflects mostly on the cheapness of Chinese labor, but it does also show the low costs of shipping."

Companies don't want to incur extra costs doing low-profit projects. Therefore, they hire outside help and give them assignments or projects when and where it is required in order to control costs. **The work that is given to people outside the company is called outsourced work, and the process is called outsourcing. Those outside individuals and companies are called freelancers or independent contractors.**

There are many companies whose core competency is in product design, and new product development and marketing. They do not manufacture their products; instead, they outsourced the work to contractors, who in turn outsourced the work at competitive prices to manufacturers in Asia and Europe, in particular China, India, and Italy.

The joy of outsourcing

TopsyTail

Many home-based businesses and microenterprises have become successful companies by outsourcing work to outside companies and manufacturers that were able to provide them with quality work at low labor costs. **Tomima Edmark,** the inventor of **"TopsyTail,"** a French-style hair accessory for women and girls, started her company, TopsyTail

Corporation, in 1991. A skillful saleswoman, she marketed her product to department stores and fashion magazines. For her business acumen and inventive skills, she received many invitations and appeared in *Forbes Magazine*, on *Good Morning America* and on *The Oprah Winfrey Show*. Sales of her product grew to $100 million in 1992. **What is interesting about her success is that instead of hiring thirty or more employees, Tomima and two workers established a network of twenty vendors and outsourced everything to them, from product manufacturing to servicing the department stores' accounts**. However, she was smart enough to keep control of the marketing strategies and new product development, the core competencies of her company.

The sorrow of outsourcing

Nike and Ikea

Many companies, such as **Nike** and **Ikea,** do not manufacture their products. They capitalized on their core competencies in product design, merchandising, and marketing, and outsourced the manufacturing segment of the work to contractors in Asia and Europe, in particular China, India, and Italy. Both companies had to issue formal apologies and make reparations to victims who were paid low wages (forced labor) to make products that those companies sold at high prices and high profit margins worldwide, especially in the United States of America.

Nike and Ikea have said their contractors and subcontractors were to blame for this atrocity. That excuse did not appease public anger, because in the court of public opinion, there are no statutes of limitations and no forgiveness if a business has committed an immoral act against the less-fortunate people in society.

Sample form

I have prepared a sample agreement form for you on the next page. Your company should have **a simple agreement form, a business policy, and a plan** that describes what kind of work you are willing to outsource to outsiders, and how you plan to do your due diligence on each contractor. Every so often we hear about companies that divulged sensitive information to contractors whom they had trusted, and lived to regret it.

I appreciate feedback from my readers and clients. My e-mail address is **ClemBarry@ aol.com**, and my website is **www.ConsultantBarry.com**.

Freelance/ Independent Contractor Agreement

(Please fill out completely)

Your name:_____

Your company name:_____

Address_____ Tel #_____

Contractor's name:_____

Tel #_____ FAX_____

E-mail_____ Website_____

SS #_____ EIN #:_____

Address:_____

City:_____ Zip:_____

Job Description_____

_____

_____

_____

Contract Price: $_____Starting Date :_____

Assignment ends: Day_____ Month_____ Yr._____

Your Signature_____ Date_____

Contractor's signature_____ Date_____

I, the undersigned contractor, hereby declare that the information above is true and correct. I further declare that I work for other companies and the assignment above will be performed by me without supervision from the owner. I am aware that I am responsible for paying my quarterly taxes and filing my tax returns.

CHAPTER 8
THE NEW WORKPLACE

Promises

Before the worldwide economic recession started in late 1993, there was an abundance of work and overtime pay for everybody who wanted to work—every able-bodied person who wanted to work. The dream of graduating from high school, technical school, polytechnic, secondary school, college, and university and getting a job that will pay a living wage or salary was more or less a guarantee.

Shattered dreams

That dream has become a virtual nightmare for many people around the world as they witness businesses downsizing their staffs and closing their operations—massive layoffs of workers on top of those workers who were previously fired plus high unemployment among former and present graduate students.

If you have been reading the major newspapers such as the *Wall Street Journal*, the *Financial Times*, *USA Today*, *Ernst & Young* reports or listening to the BBC, Euro-News, or Blumberg News, you will conclude that times have changed and the world economy has certainly changed.

Speculation is rife that holding on to a permanent job from the cradle to the grave, in the private and public sector, has become a thing of the past, as there are no present or future guarantees that anybody who has a job today will have the same job tomorrow.

The opinion of many economists, employers, and labor statisticians is that it would take many years before this huge backlog of job seekers would get employment in the private and public services sectors.

Self-determination

The worldwide economic recession has changed the job market in every industry, and it has presented new challenges, opportunities, and greater competition for people in every country. Hence, this large pool of unemployed people will have to consider doing one of the following:

1. Start their own businesses from their homes and get outsourced work from large contractors while they build a strong customer or client base
2. Start their own businesses from their homes and get outsourced work from their former employers while they build a strong customer or client base
3. Buy an existing business
4. Buy a franchise

Some people have started their own business with the hope of getting a job when the economy rebounds and the job market improves. That sounds plausible, but some of them may not have the marketable skills that employers will be looking for in new applicants, and many of them may reach retirement age before the economy rebounds and companies began hiring higher-paid workers.

The private sector

Private sector downsizing and outsourcing of work in the aftermath of the worldwide economic recession that started in 2006 will continue for many years. Employers will make it a policy to do more with less as they continue to streamline their operations. They will continue to use modern technology and outsourcing to maximize productivity, keep costs down, and compete against cheaper imports, clones, and products that are smuggled into their country.

Here is an excerpt from an article that I have read on the Internet. The sole purpose of reproducing the article here is to illustrate my points about what is happening in the real world and what the backlog of unemployed people will be facing in the future.

"Employer explains why he won't hire the unemployed"
AOL Jobs; By Claire Gordon; posted Oct 12, 2012.

Discrimination against the unemployed is rampant. Some advertisements for jobs have explicitly stated that applicants must be "Currently Employed." Some people who have been out of work for a year or longer have reported that prospective employers have rejected them as soon as they mentioned that they are unemployed.

Why are employers averse to hiring the jobless? AOL Jobs called about a half dozen employers who took out ads that explicitly stated that current employment was required of all applicants. However, only one employer, Alex Comana had agreed to be interviewed. He operates the Comana Company, a property management and real estate firm in La Mesa, California. He is seeking to hire an apartment complex manager. He had posted a job offering to fill that position and it specified that only currently employed individuals need apply.

Here are some of the reasons he has given:

1. People who have a job are proven to be valuable.
2. You can't be sure why the unemployed lost their jobs.
3. The employed will adjust quicker to a new job.
4. An employed candidate has fresher job skills.

The economy

Downsizing will continue as countries around the world continue to feel the wrath and the aftermath of the worldwide economic recession. **People who were laid off, terminated, or dismissed from their jobs will continue to have difficulties finding employment as their countries grapple with financial constraints in the absence of economic growth, and as those countries succumbed to credit downgrading from Standard & Poor's and Fitch and Moody's, and tough austerity measures or**

economic reforms by the IMF and other lending institutions as foreign aids (grants and gifts from donor countries), remittances from citizens abroad, and foreign direct investments dwindle or slow to a trickle.

Hugh debts

Huge, growing, or uncontrollable debts in businesses and countries do have adverse effects on business and economic growth, as well as on economic and social stability and security. As interest payments continue to diminish the net incomes of businesses and the GDP of countries, those businesses and countries will continue to have less and less money available to invest in research, innovation, and infrastructure development. In addition, there is the risk that those businesses and countries would not be able to pay workers and creditors.

The result is layoffs of workers, dissolution of the businesses, a steady reduction in income and sales tax (VAT), high unemployment, crime, crumbling infrastructure, and a steady reduction in foreign investments and tourism. This has spurred demonstrations, riots, and political destabilization in many countries as citizens continue to have difficulties meeting their basic needs and steadily lose confidence for a better future.

Summary

The worldwide economic recession was a wakeup call for political leaders in every country. It has made them look at the world in a different light as international lenders and financial regulatory institutions such as the IMF, the World Bank, and the European Community Bank push austerity measures on them and force them to reform their economies and make their countries competitive.

The United Kingdom, Greece, Brazil, and many other countries had only cared about big businesses and foreign direct investments. With the exception of Germany, which subsidizes SMEs and small businesses in the arts and sciences, most of the G-20 countries had turned a blind eye on SMEs, microenterprise, and entrepreneurship. **Small-business applicants had to sometimes wait for three years before those**

countries would approve their business applications or grant them a permit or license to operate.

Politicians' backs are against the wall, and they are scrambling to balance their budgets, maintain financial or fiscal stability, pay government or civil service workers, and reduce unemployment. Hence, they are encouraging nationals to start their own businesses as an alternative for reducing unemployment. **They are changing their rules to speed up business registrations, permits, and licensing approvals in order to manage the underground economy and collect billions of dollars in business registration fees, licensing fees, sales tax (VAT), and income taxes from street vendors and entrepreneurs**.

I appreciate feedback from my readers and clients. My e-mail address is **ClemBarry@ aol.com**, and my website is **www.ConsultantBarry.com**.

CHAPTER 9
CHOICE OF INDUSTRY

When I graduated from secondary school and was searching for my first job, two seasoned professionals told me:

1. "A lot of people go through life hating what they do for a living. Find something that you enjoy doing, because you will be working for most of your life."
2. "Find something that you enjoy and excel in, that other people don't like to do. People will always pay someone else to do what they don't like doing."

"Respect doesn't come from the kind of work you do; it comes from the way you do the work." —Kenneth L. Shipley

Everybody cannot do the same job because talents and aspirations vary. If everybody does the same job, economic growth will stagnate, and many of us would not be alive. Hence, vibrant economic activities and economic growth can only come from a diverse labor force that is comprised of people in different trades and professions. I call that **"economic empowerment."**

There is a saying: **"If you like what you do, you will never work a day in your life."** Chris Gardner, a homeless man who became a millionaire, has a very simple philosophy. He says the secret to his success is, **"Find something you love to do so much that you can't wait for the sun to rise to do it all over again."** This brings me to my next point. Colonel Sanders, the founder of KFC; Sam Walton, the founder of Walmart; Steve Jobs from Apple Computer; and several other entrepreneurs had so much love for what they were doing that they literally died on the job. They retired when they were about to die.

Do you believe Warren Buffett, Richard Branson, Mark Zuckerberg, Michael Dell, Bill Gates, Oprah Winfrey, and other first-generation entrepreneurs would retire from their companies? They may step aside and hire another person to manage their businesses, but they will not retire or divorce themselves from the companies that they have built. I know retired business owners who came out of retirement and went back to work and revived their companies. They just could not sit back and watch their companies collapse.

Choosing an industry that you would like to work in is similar to choosing a career path. **If you choose the right industry, you will be happy to come to work every day**.

When you are in charge of your own business, you have a say about how your service is offered and delivered to the public or how your product is manufactured, how it looks, how it is packaged, how it is distributed, and where it is sold. You are really enjoying what you are doing. You are able to do the things that you could not get the opportunity to do when you worked for someone else's company, where your role was clearly defined, and you did not have a lot of creative input and flexibility.

You have read success stories about great entrepreneurs, and you are motivated to start you own business and make a name for yourself. However, before you start a business in an industry that you are passionate about, you must be able to demonstrate some basic character traits or hire people who have them.

1. **Training:** You can take classes, attend seminars and group meetings, or hire a mentor or trainer who understands your business and the industry in which it operates.

2. **Knowledge:** It is important that you have experience working part time or full time in the industry. Avoid getting into a cash crisis by understanding financial or cash management and the nature or seasonality of your industry. Cash is king; therefore, a shortage of working capital to operate your business can be emotionally devastating for you, and it can force you to close your business. You must understand and comply with income tax rules and employment tax rules and be thorough about the product or service that you will sell to customers. You will be competing against experienced business owners, and customers will be delighted to patronize your business if you are resourceful.

3. **Confidence:** You must demonstrate confidence in the product and service that you are selling. If you are not confident in your abilities and the product and services that you are selling, then why should customers trust you?

4. **Discipline:** As a business owner, you must be passionate about your business, focused, detail oriented, and resilient. You must demonstrate your full commitment to the business; otherwise, stakeholders—lenders, investors, customers, suppliers, and employees—will not take you seriously.

5. **Ethics:** Honesty is the best policy. Customers, suppliers, and investors want to do business with people who are credible or honest and who can give them that level of assurance. **Successful business owners demonstrate credibility by honoring their obligations and being candid with their stakeholders—customers, suppliers, employees, investors, etc**. Here is a true story. A well-known beer company had supplied a vendor with beer on consignment (without a down payment). The vendor sent the beer company several checks that bounced or were dishonored by the bank. After warning the vendor every time the incident occurred, the credit supervisor at the beer company got disheartened and reported the matter to the police department in January 2008. The vendor was on the run for two years, dodging subpoenas and hiding from the police. The police fraud squad arrested the vendor in November 2010. The vendor pleaded not guilty and was given bail. The case was called and adjourned several times. In February 2013, the vendor was sentenced to pay restitution and is serving three years in prison.

6. **Team worker:** Whether you hire employees or delegate work to outsourced companies, you must be willing to work with other people as a team and give credit and recognition to teams and team members and make everybody feel important.

7. **Enthusiasm:** Howard Schultz, the founder and inspirational and courageous cheerleader of Starbucks has said, **"I am always energized to come to work every day."** Competing against top challengers such as McDonald's and Dunkin' Donuts in a highly competitive coffee industry, Schultz has taken nothing for granted in his quest to continue to enhance the Starbucks experience and create more avenues for growth. He scouts the world to get the best-grown coffee beans, pays farmers to produce special coffee beans for his company, and built a special roaster to roast and blend the coffee beans to meet the taste and aroma to which his customers have become accustomed. **In his quest to grow his company, he went as far as forming an alliance or strategic partnership**

with competitor Green Mountain Coffee. That was a smart business move for three reasons:

a. **Strategic partnering is sometimes important because lack of collaboration can breed destructive competition, and I don't think he wants to rock the boat or shake the apple cart. Sometimes it pays to be friendly to your competitor.**
b. **Both companies were at their best when they competed against each other, and they are also at their best when they joined as strategic partners.**
c. **Some of the patent held by Green Mountain Coffee will soon expire, and Schultz is poised to benefit from that, although the executives at Green Mountain Coffee have said they were not overly concerned about that.**

I have followed the careers of people who have done very well in business, and I have noticed that they have demonstrated certain character traits. They are innovative, and they keep their customers and audiences motivated and captivated by doing what they do best, and doing it with enthusiasm and staying ahead of the competition.

Vince McMahon was able to take the WWF, now called the WWE, from a start-up to a publicly traded company because he was passionate about the business, and he knew how to combine, present, and promote the skills of his wrestlers with dramatic story lines that are plausible and exciting to the fans. He knows how to thrill the fans, schedule and announce the events months in advance, price the tickets and merchandise right, and sell out arenas weeks in advance.

Dana White has taken the UFC from the brink of collapse, or near bankruptcy, and turned it around and made it an international brand by booking skilled kick boxers who are passionate and dedicated to the sport, and using unconventional but savvy management skills to differentiate the UFC from the WWE. Many savvy businessmen with a lot of money have tried to copy his model and have failed.

CHAPTER 10
PRODUCT OR SERVICE

"Quality is never an accident; it is always the result of intelligent effort."
—John Ruskin

1. Define your product or service

a. A company that sells a range of products should have at least one product that defines and uplifts other products in the brand. That product should be the star in the company's booth at trade shows, on supermarket shelves, in showrooms, on brochures, and on its website. Rolex brand of watches consists of several kinds of watches, and they vary in price, but the company markets its watches around its superstar, the $40,000 Submariner brand. Mercedes Benz markets its cars around its superstar, the E63 AMG; and Audi uses the new R8.

b. A company that sells a range of services should have at least one service that defines and uplifts other services in the brand. That one service should be the star on its business card, brochure, and website.

2. Packaging

The packaging of your product or service is the image you want to convey that would influence the purchasing decision of your target customers or target market. Packaging is a combination of the things that your customers see and the benefits they envision they will receive, or the satisfaction they will enjoy when they purchase and use your product or service.

The whole package, or the total package, includes the design and quality of your promotional items, such as wrapping paper, bottles, boxes, file folders, and shopping bags. The benefits, or satisfaction, include product performance, user experience, return policy, guarantees, warrantees, and customer service experience. Everything must be in harmony with the equity of the brand, or everything must be grounded in the equity of the brand, or everything must be enshrined in the equity of the brand. Please note that I did not mention anything about price, because you are not competing on price. You are selling customer experience and customer satisfaction, which are everything nowadays.

3. Branding

When you are planning what hotel to book for a family vacation, a different image will come to mind when you are considering Motel 6 versus Hilton, Ritz-Carlton versus Days Inn, Hotel California versus Marriott, or the Four Seasons versus Double Tree hotels versus the Embassy Suites hotels. Each hotel has conveyed two impressions:

  a. The caliber or quality of the hotel
  b. The price of the hotel

Those are two of the characteristics that identify or distinguish the hotel brands. They act as the basis or standard that customers would use to place their faith and confidence in other establishments, such as restaurants, banks, airlines, law firms, insurance companies, and accounting firms.

What is a brand?

A brand is more than a name and a logo. It is a promise of service, quality, safety, value, consistency, and accountability. Brands have a recognizable style, language, and consistent message. Anything less is a flawed reason and an inherent danger to consider a product or service as a brand.

Branded Individuals

"Your brand is what your customers think of you, not what you think of yourself." —Jon Taffer, Bar Rescue.

Branded items demonstrate excellence in product and service quality. The same is true for branded individuals. However, for branded individuals, and individuals who endorse brands, we must add character traits such as, benefits, personality, loyalty, ethics, and integrity. In branding, whatever a representative says and how she or he communicates the information can boost or hurt the integrity of the brand. That person's language and personality are integral to the brand, hence the reason why brands include the following clause into their contracts:

"We expect those that represent us to exhibit their best behavior at all times. We hold our partners to a high standard, and we expect them to live up to the values of our brand."

The purpose of brands

Brands instill confidence in consumers' purchasing decisions. Consumers have choices and preferences, and they want to buy with confidence. Hence, they usually purchase products and services from names that they know and trust. For example, when a consumer buys a product from BMW, Mercedes, Rolex, General Electric, Shell, and Exxon, the consumer has signaled to those companies that he or she has placed trust and faith in their ideas, thoughts, discernment, and judgment, and wants to enjoy a comfortable and memorable relationship with the product.

Brand improvement

Just like everything else in life, brands cannot be static. They must continuously revamp and reposition themselves to their current and prospective customers. Kodak did not keep up with innovation and economic and market trends; hence, its demise. Rolls Royce and other high-end brands seldom advertise because overexposure can hurt the value of those brands. Brands are elite products and services. There are people who would purchase products and services that are exclusive, and they will pay a premium for the peace of mind that comes with them—the value exceeds the costs.

4. Reliability

Errors and mistakes occur in spite of a manufacturer's best efforts to produce a quality and safe product. Product quality and safety control methods should constantly be reviewed and adjusted by the manufacturer, and monitored by the distributor and retailer from feedback they received from customers. Hence, random testing and regular inspections of your product would help you identify and manage breaches in product quality and safety.

An unsafe product should be recalled before it becomes a public safety issue and diminishes the sales volume and value of your brand. Unsuspecting consumers did not contaminate or tamper with the product; therefore, manufacturers, distributors, and retailers can be held jointly and severally liable for compromising consumers' health and safety for profit.

Faced with issues about product tampering in 1982, Johnson & Johnson was forced to recall all capsules of its biggest seller, **Tylenol**, from the market. In August 2012, 1,039 cases of bagged **Dole** Fresh Vegetables salad were voluntarily recalled. The recall notification was issued because of an isolated instance of contamination, in which a sample of Dole Italian Blend salad yielded a positive result for listeria monocytogenes in a random sample test conducted by the North Carolina Department of Agriculture. However, no sickness was reported in association with the recall.

In February 2013, **Nestle** suspended deliveries and recalled all its products that include beef from its German supplier because "traces of horse DNA" were discovered in a variety of products labeled as beef that were sold in supermarkets in Britain, Ireland, Germany, Sweden, Switzerland, and France. Protest against biotech giant **Monsanto** for compromising public health began in February 2013, and it grew in March 2013 to over two million people in fifty countries. Consumers were fearful that the company was compromising their health using genetically modified seeds to increase farm and food productivity. However, Monsanto argues that several tests by scientists and the US government have shown its products are safe for human consumption.

5. Core competence

The core competence of a company is the strength or competitive edge the company has in the marketplace. Core competence has three main characteristics:

a. It is a source of competitive advantage.
b. It has a breadth of application.
c. It is not easily copied or imitated.

Why are Exxon, Rolex, Hilton Hotels, and Sandals Resorts considered number one in their respective industries? Why are Barnes & Noble, Walmart, Dell, and Microsoft considered number one in their respective markets? The answer is that those companies have distinct advantages that they skillfully blend together to attract and retain customers. Each company in each industry possesses distinctive capabilities and resources that it skillfully integrates to pique the interest and satisfy the motives of customers in the market it targets and serves.

Apart from not having a monopoly in the marketplace, high-quality service would definitely distinguish your business from your competitors'. Your interpersonal and communication skills, coupled with your honesty about your product or service and your relationship with your customers, are things that your competitors cannot monitor or easily duplicate. Business owners will usually go above and beyond their service policy to accommodate their customers. Therefore, competitors can only speculate about the kind of service that you will provide to a typical customer on a typical day, since customers' needs and preferences change like the weather; hence, the reason why high-priced brands such as Mercedes Benz, BMW, Rolex, and others are flourishing.

6. Value

a. Why do people camp out for many hours, and sometimes in inclement weather conditions, to buy concert tickets, Nike sneakers, and Apple phones?
b. Why do tickets for concerts and movies sell out in minutes after the names of certain entertainers, bands, movies, etc., are mentioned?

Whenever we tell consumers that they would receive the best value for their money, we are saying to them that "they will receive the best value in terms of quality, innovation, delivery, support service, and results or satisfaction." Please note that price was not mentioned here, because we are not competing on price. We are selling value. Value pricing in a service industry such as law, insurance, finance, accounting, and taxation is based on results (performance-based compensation). It is a percentage of what these professionals have saved their clients.

Value is not what we put into a product or service. It is the benefit that the customer gets out of it after they pay for it.

    a. **Value = Benefit – Cost**
    b. **Benefit = Value – Cost**

You must demonstrate to prospective customers that using your product or service will increase their revenue or cut their cost or give them peace of mind. If the product or service provides the customer with greater peace of mind, then the customer benefits. What you should be concerned about and what should matter most to customers who buy your product or service is the financial, emotional, physical, or spiritual benefit that your product or service provides them.

7. Price

"You can price yourself out of the market by selling too high, or price yourself out of business by selling too low."

Customers don't care about how much money you spent to provide them with a service or product. Their only concern is what they feel they should pay for your service or product; and most of the time what they want to pay are ridiculously low prices that would certainly put you out of business.

Your responsibility is to develop a strong business model and a profitable and realistic pricing method to help your company overcome price pressure and price wars. Reducing prices to increase sales or to encourage new customers to buy can reduce your **margin of safety** (see glossary for explanation). Most importantly, it usually sends the wrong message that something is wrong with your product or service, or maybe you don't have confidence in your product or service.

Every business is responsible to meet its financial obligations. Your business should be able to exert sufficient pricing power to meet its financial goals by bringing together the right mix of products or services, and by emphasizing quality, durability, business culture, customer service, integrity, and reliability in every transaction.

Target stores have competed on prices for many years. They are leaders in price cutting. However, in October 2012, company officials made a shocking public announcement that the stores would not be reducing prices in December 2012, during the Christmas shopping season. The reason company officials cited was that the stores could no longer prolong the price-cutting war. Cutting prices further would jeopardize the stores' survival.

Price-conscious consumers were angry when the announcement was made, and they have threatened to shop elsewhere and never return to shop at Target stores. However, there were consumers who agreed with Target's decision and promised to continue to shop at the stores. Some of them have said they have instructed their stockbrokers to buy Target's shares of stock for them.

In my opinion, Target had finally found the **profitability curve**—competitive prices that would produce the most sales and maximum profit per item. They have learned from losses that they have suffered in previous price wars, and they are trying to recoup loss profits by adapting and adhering to a more disciplined business practice. Management at the company must have realized that their industry was destroying itself by following misguided practices such as unnecessary price wars.

Some business owners have told me if they don't follow their competitors and reduce their price, they would lose the sale. My advice is, don't fall for that. Consumers may become more price-sensitive if they are worrying about the economy, job security, and the future. However, that does not mean consumers have changed psychologically in terms of their perception of value.

Many of them who are insisting on paying low prices for your products would still shop at **Tiffany**, **Ralph Lauren**, and **Tommy Hilfiger** and pay premium prices for similar items they could have bought cheaper elsewhere. If a company reacts too quickly and lowers prices to match competitors' prices, then the public or stakeholders will assume that the company's prices were too high in the first place, and it was gouging consumers, or the company is just following the crowd without knowing if its competitors are operating profitably, just breaking even, or selling below costs. Please be aware that there are companies that would sell some of their products below cost (lost leaders) to lure unsuspecting consumers to buy other expensive products.

There are products that consumers would buy only if they are on sale—consumers treat them as just another **commodity item** with little or no **intrinsic value**. However, there are products those same consumers would pay premium prices for because those products are **brand items**, and consumers have had a memorable experience with those products. Hence, they have different expectations for the same product. For example, a bottle of generic or supermarket brand ketchup may sell for 20 percent less than a bottle of Heinz ketchup, but customers would still put a bottle of Heinz ketchup in their shopping carts. Similarly, a can of supermarket corned beef may sell for 15 percent less than a can of Libby's corned beef, but consumers would still put a can of Libby's corned beef in their shopping carts because consumers have different expectations for the same product. The same thing can be said about:

a. **Rolex versus Swatch**
b. **Hotel California versus Motel 6**
c. **Nestlé versus condensed milk**
d. **Organic food versus natural food**

Sure, buyers are price conscious; and you should be too as a business owner because you do not want to price yourself out of the market. Sure, buyers care about price, but they also evaluate other attributes, such as proximity to the location of the store, customer service, product or service quality, product durability, return policy, no restocking fee, better warranty protection, and the overall perception or experience of doing business with a company when they are gauging or estimating the reasonableness of paying a certain price.

8. Shoplifting

There was a time when people respected other people's property, and they would seldom take other people's property without their permission. The slogan was, **"If it does not belong to you, don't touch it."** Today, the mind-set of many people is, **"If you don't protect it, don't blame us for stealing it."** Hence, shoplifting has become the norm, and store owners are responding by protecting their suppliers (fiduciary trust) without scaring potential customers. This includes locking glass showcases that contain expensive products, installing alarms on merchandise, installing security cameras around their stores, hiring security personnel to monitor those cameras, and escorting shoplifters quietly back to the stores, where they would plead guilty, sign waivers, pose for their photograph to be taken, and be released with a warning that they will be arrested if they return to the stores, and they are caught shoplifting.

Employees at those stores depend on their store's success so that they can earn a livelihood, and governments depend on the sales from those stores to collect employment and sales taxes. Suppliers, creditors, and outsourcing companies are owed money by those stores, and they are helping those stores to become successful so that they too will continue to be in business. Hence, shoplifting has a domino effect on everybody in the food chain. A small business can expect to lose $1,000 a week in stolen merchandise; and during tough economic times when disposable income is scarce, shoplifters have put many small businesses out of business. As a certified fraud examiner (CFE), and an insurance broker, I have worked with several store managers and loss prevention specialists, so I understand how the schemes work.

Why do people shoplift?

a. They want something for free.
b. They need to support an addiction.
c. They like the thrill (thrill seekers).
d. They are **boosters**—professional shoplifters that supply "**fences**" with stolen merchandise to be delivered to distributors.

What are their methodologies?

a. They come into the stores holding empty shopping bags from other stores. They remove the alarm tags from merchandise in the store and load the merchandise into their bags and boldly walk out of the store **(fencing)**.

b. They switch the price tags with lower price tags and pay less for the merchandise **(price switching)**.

c. They walk into the store drinking soda or coffee from a straw in a coffee cup. They remove the lid from the cup and drop an item of jewelry into the soda or coffee. They replace the lid on the cup and pretend they are drinking from the straw and boldly walk out the door **(concealment)**.

d. They take an item of clothing into the dressing room and remove the alarm tag and label from it. They put on the new garment in the dressing room and leave their old garment behind **(garment switching)**.

e. They pay employees to sneak stolen merchandise into a trash can or garbage container outside the store, or have employees carry stolen merchandise in the store shopping bags or boxes to their cars in the parking lot **(coconspiracy)**.

f. They bring back the stolen merchandise and ask for cash **(refund fraud)**. According to industry estimates, consumers return over $200 billion worth of merchandise annually, or almost 8 percent of total retail sales.

Retailers are fighting back

1. Some stores are insisting that all customers leave their shopping bags and containers with the security guard. A tag number is attached to the container, and the same tag number is given to the customer to reclaim his or her property on the way out of the store.

2. The height of the shelves, racks, and pallets in the aisles is lower. This allows more visibility throughout the store.

3. Brighter energy-efficient lights are installed throughout the store.

4. More visible and hidden security cameras are installed and monitored throughout the store.

5. The retail industry has compiled a database with the names of people who frequently return merchandise. Your name may be in that database if you have ever returned merchandise to a retail store. The data keeps merchandisers and stores informed about **"chronic returners"** and gangs of thieves who are trying

to get cash or store credit for merchandize they returned. This practice has led to a privacy lawsuit by a customer against Best Buy Corp. However, the lawsuit was dismissed for lack of merit.

A return tracking company, The Retail Equation, in California, says it does not share information that it complies for its clients. For example, if it compiles a merchandise return activity about customers who have returned Playtex's merchandise, it would report the information to Playtex alone. Victoria's Secret would not be privy to the information.

I appreciate feedback from my readers and clients. My e-mail address is **ClemBarry@ aol.com**, and my website is **www.ConsultantBarry.com**.

CHAPTER 11
COMPETITION

Business owners in the United States of America are market savvy, and they are very competitive and aggressive. If you become too complacent, you will lose market share quickly to competitors with aggressive marketing techniques.

A company is more likely to be outwitted by emerging competitors (new entrants) and new technologies than by its existing competitors.

Eastman Kodak: Kodak was in the film business. Instead of listening to its customers and focusing on customers' needs, management at Kodak wasted time worrying about its closest competitor, Fuji Films. Kodak did not foresee the long-term erosion of its market by filmless cameras that emerging competitors Cannon and Sony were bringing into the market. Kodak went into bankruptcy and receivership because management held tightly to old business methods when they should have been innovating to meet customers' demands. A lot of photography stores that depended on Kodak have lost their businesses to Cannon, Sony, and new entrants in the new, competitive environment. That can happen in any industry.

One of the key elements for business survival and growth is the ability of a company's management team to keep their products and services relevant in a changing market economy. This can be accomplished by carefully listening to the advice of their salespeople and accurately predicting future changes in the business environment and constantly modifying their business model or operating strategies to adapt to changes in economic and market trends.

Montgomery Ward & Company: For many years it was one of the leading department and mail-order retail stores in the United States of America. It did not respond quickly to changes in the demographics of the population and a changing US economy. Competitors such as, Sears, JC Penny, Macy's, and Dillard's department stores responded quickly to the changes and eroded its market share. Soon those stores began to lose market share to low-price or discount competitors such as Kmart, Target, and Walmart, which also captured more market share from Montgomery Ward. Finally, Montgomery Ward filed for bankruptcy and went out of business in 2000. Kmart filed for bankruptcy and business reorganization several years later, reformed or restructured its operations, and emerged from bankruptcy with a fresh start.

An Wang started Wang Laboratories in a rented room above a garage in Boston, USA. The company earned close to $15,000 in the first year of operation. Its products were an instant hit with large companies, and Wang Laboratories grew 35 percent per year. Its annual sales skyrocketed to $2 billion, and profits reached $200 million. Wang hardware and software were not compatible with those that were made by other companies. The company's proprietary strategy locked in customers and earned Wang high profit margins. Customers began asking for an "open system" that would have made Wang systems compatible with other systems. Wang became stubborn, refused to listen to them, and refused to change. Customers began migrating to other companies, and Wang eventually filed for bankruptcy. It emerged from bankruptcy one year later, but rapidly changing technology had made its computers obsolete (high-tech relics). The new CEO had to convince/persuade existing customers to remain with the company, transformed the company into a fast-paced consultancy service provider, and struggled to overcome the stigma or taint of bankruptcy.

Compaq computer was a success story. The company had carved out a niche with its high-margin, state of the art computers and had steady growth and great success for many years. Samsung and Packard-Bell entered the market with cheaper clones that were selling in discount stores and catalogs. In addition, Samsung and Packard-Bell were providing the same quality parts and sometimes higher-quality parts faster and cheaper than those from Compaq's factory and its suppliers. Customers' preferences changed, and they started to buy the cheaper clones that were made by Samsung and Packard-Bell. Compaq's market had changed, and company executives were slow to react to the changes. Soon the company was on the verge of extinction. It rebounded after company executives reexamined consumers' needs and redefined the attributes that the company and its products must provide to consumers to regain its market share.

Those changes are not unique to technology companies. Rather, they reflect fundamental changes in the way companies must design, build, market, and sell products as consumers' preferences and markets change.

When **Napster** and other music pirates started selling music over the Internet to herds of young fans, record companies were slow to adapt to the sudden shift in demands. Many companies that had depended on Sony lost their customer and went out of business. Today, Sony Corporation is still struggling to cope with the sudden change in demand.

Tobacco companies and distributors that sell expensive tobacco and cigars must revisit their business model because barriers to entry into their markets are now lowered. There is a cultural shift in the marketplace. People can buy substitutes, such as legalized marijuana, in the states of Massachusetts, Colorado, California, Louisiana, and Washington, and in Philadelphia, because the laws governing marijuana in those states have become more relaxed.

Competitors are getting more aggressive in their marketing programs and in the marketplace. They are spending a lot of money on research and development (R&D) and business consultation in order to improve their products, increase market share, and increase shareholders' returns. Be alert and continue to monitor changes in the marketplace. Products and services that are in demand and selling like hotcakes will have to compete with new products, substitute products, cheaper imported products, and exceptional services.

CHAPTER 12

BUSINESS ADVISORS

I am sure you are familiar with the proverb, "You are as good as the people you hire."

Focus your time and energy on doing those things that you are good at, and hire qualified people to handle the rest. Every business is designed so that each aspect of the work flow is handled by a knowledgeable person, in-house or outsourced. Of course, one person in your company may be capable of wearing several hats. However, be prepared and be happy to outsource work that you and your employees cannot handle.

Here are two examples that clarify what I am talking about:

1. I am knowledgeable about marketing, website design, and computer technology. I can manage my website by myself, but instead I outsource the work to a marketing company that specializes in doing marketing for accountants. I have been with them for over eighteen years.
2. I have a master's degree in taxation, and I can do tax research myself. I am too busy to do the tax research myself, so I pay monthly fees to two tax research companies to do the research for me. I have been with those companies for over twenty years.

Here are the advantages:

a. I am doing my clients a great service by obtaining up-to-date tax information from two recognized and reliable sources.
b. Those company have done excellent work for me.

97

c. The benefits have always been greater than the costs.

d. The cost of their services is a tax break that is deductible on my business tax returns.

Your advisors are good resources that you can tap into whenever you are stuck with a business decision. They should be able to give you the proper advice that you need to operate your business efficiently and the guidance that you need to implement that advice and build your business.

Business advisors that a business owner would have to consult with are: banker, attorney, accountant, tax advisor, suppliers, investors, etc. Your business advisors should be people whom you trust based on your experience with them. A rule of thumb is to do your due diligence on everybody whom you planned to surround yourself with, then choose the best advisors and form an advisory board and hold monthly or quarterly business review meetings with your board.

Brian Hamilton, cofounder and CEO of Sage-Works Inc., has summarized it this way, at the conclusion of his interview with *Inc.* magazine in August 2011: **"You need to surround yourself with people who can help you, and those people will or should be people who won't always agree with you. For this reason, all businesses, no matter the size, should have an outside Board of Directors or group to advise the entrepreneur."**

Barry's Accounting Services Corporation provides custom-made consultation services for entrepreneurships, corporations, and mid- to high-income individuals. Clients can choose from an array of value-added services covering fifteen industries, plus other key services such as expertise in debt control and cash management, cost segregation, activity-based costing, transfer pricing, revenue acceleration, and extensive experience in due diligence, forensic accounting, business reorganization/restructuring, property and casualty insurance claims, construction contracts, and procurement. Log on to our website, **www.ConsultantBarry.com**

I appreciate feedback from my readers and clients. My e-mail address is **ClemBarry@aol.com**, and my website is **www.ConsultantBarry.com**.

CHAPTER 13
BUSINESS CONSULTANTS

Who Is a consultant?

A business consultant is an individual that is resourceful, possesses in-depth knowledge about solving business problems in a particular industry or several industries, and has a track record of helping people transform their ambition to achievement.

Why would anyone need a consultant?

Fact No. 1

There are many people with dreams, goals, and brilliant ideas. They have a burning desire to turn their dreams into reality—into hot commodities or into products or services that create demand. Usually, they would turn to someone with a business background and entrepreneurial savvy to help them transform their thoughts and focus on what matters the most—accomplishing their objectives.

Fact No. 2

Companies frequently seek help from outside professionals because they want a different prospective or a fresh/new approach to finding a solution to a problem. Also because it is sometimes more feasible for them to do so than to retain in-house specialists in every discipline in which expertise is required.

Fact No. 3

Independent consultants can, and they sometimes do, revive ailing companies and save jobs during economic recessions, when everybody is running away from those companies. Some consultants broker financial and bailout deals to keep companies out of bankruptcy court or receivership. Some of them have invested their own money in companies that have given them a warranty and the authority to restructure/reform and manage them.

Fact No. 4

An investigation that involves allegations against executives; or issues that have an impact on a company's operation, finances, value, reputation, or validity as a going concern would have to be conducted by outside professionals—independent consultants that do not have close ties to the company because the findings/results must be beyond reproach.

Services consultants provide

1. Cash flow management

"Everything feels better when cash inflow exceeds cash outflow."

Most business failure is due to a lack of working capital (daily shortage of cash). Negative cash flow can be emotionally devastating to a business owner. A business owner who wants to avoid a cash flow problem should develop a daily and weekly cash flow projection to meet and manage the business needs. Oftentimes, business owners are vague or confused about what has happened to the money that they have collected for the business. A historical cash flow statement can be prepared to help the business owner understand how the money was collected and how it was spent (sources and application of funds). The business owner can also get help with:

 a. Obtaining an appropriate line of credit/overdraft
 b. Setting up an effective credit and collection policy
 c. Setting up an effective payment policy
 d. Obtaining the maximum rate of return on idle cash

2. Strategic business planning

Failure to provide an accurate picture of a situation would slow a business's ability to capitalize on an opportunity or fix a problem.

A business plan and the related or associated documents can tell a lot about the strategies and assumptions of a successful or a failed company. If you are familiar with the industry that a successful or a failed company operated in, then you can look at those documents and ask yourself a lot of important questions.

A **strategic business plan** helps a business owner to clarify the direction of the business, ensure divisional or departmental leaders or managers are focusing on key issues, and keeps management and employees focused on the projects and tasks at hand.

3. Business valuation

Business valuation is the appraisal of the economic value of a business.

Who would need a business valuation report?

Buyers, partners, courts, taxing authorities, creditors, and investors need the report.

When is a business valuation report required?

1. Buying, merging, or selling a business
2. Divorce proceedings
3. Estate planning and probate
4. Partner(s) entering and exiting
5. Filing for bankruptcy and reorganization
6. Tax purposes (evaluating capital gains or losses)
7. Verification of worth (bankers and investors)
8. Private placement and initial public offering

When will the report be available?

From three days to ninety days—it depends on how quickly you provide us with the necessary information, how quickly we can have access to the business, and how quickly you pay us.

4. Business turnaround

There is no bigger challenge in business than successfully completing a business turnaround or restructuring. All restructuring starts with the people who work for the company:

a. How they manage the business
b. How they communicate
c. How they serve the customers

The companies that we have turned around had the classic problem of having their costs higher than their revenue trajectory. Transformation of a company that is in a financial crisis involves stabilizing the company quickly and charting a long-term course for growth.

5. Forensic investigation and due diligence test

Forensic accountants are frequently contacted and hired by taxpayers involved in alleged tax evasion cases. They are seeking a recommendation on how they should proceed and want to know the laws governing the issues raised in the case. Some people hire forensic accountants when they have strong suspicion that a trusted representative is fleecing their investment account(s); when their business is hemorrhaging money, and they are uncertain who is siphoning the money out of the business; to evaluate a franchisor's offering circular and franchise agreement; or to evaluate equitable distribution in business and marital dissolution when a spouse or business partner feels cheated out of his/her fair share.

Forensic accountants add credibility to financial investigations. They are hired by corporations to boost shareholder confidence when a whistle-blower informs management about employee embezzlement, skimming, theft of merchandise, ghost vendors, inflated invoices by contractors, employees acting in collusion with vendors and customers, diversion of merchandise by the purchasing and receiving departments, and waste and abuses, or when the internal auditors discovered inaccuracies and irregularities (anomalies) in the company's books, records, and source documents, and unexplained changes in the financial statement that represent fraud symptoms that must be investigated (earnings manipulation).

Barry's Accounting Services Corporation is a certified management consulting company that provides service to small and medium-size companies. Log on to our website at **www.ConsultantBarry.com.**

CHAPTER 14
BUSINESS PLANNING

The business plan

Every business owner has one minute to attract an investor's attention and make a lasting impression. Your business plan should be simple, clear, factual, interesting, and exciting. Write your business plan so that investors can read it, follow it, understand it, and relate to it.

I am sure you are familiar with the following proverbial sayings:

1. **"You can't set the course for where you are going until you know where you are."**
2. **"Those who've failed to plan have planned to fail."**
3. **"If you shoot for the stars and miss, you would at least get to the moon."**

Many businesses operating today were launched in the middle of the economic recession in 2008. Those businesses were able to survive during the economic recession because they had a strong and realistic business plan that the owners skillfully executed in a timely manner. **Execution is the discipline to get things done. It is the opposite of procrastination.**

"A perfect plan that takes too long to execute will fail, but a good plan executed vigorously will carry the day." —General Patton, US Army.

1. A carefully prepared business plan will help you clarify your company's vision and direction, keep managers and employees focused on the goals and tasks

at hand; and ensure that project leaders are held accountable for making bad decisions.

2. A business plan should be written before the business is started, and it should be reviewed and modified periodically during the life of the business.

3. Do not talk to lenders and potential investors if you don't have a realistic business plan.

4. You should have a clear vision about what you want to accomplish. Your plan should be written. It should be coherent and easy to follow, and it should communicate passion and purpose. Your plan should be modified to suit changes in the company, changes in economic and market trends, or changes in the demographics of the population.

5. A business plan is comprised of several important segments.

    a. The mission statement
    b. Executive summary
    c. Cash budgets and financial statements
    d. Owners' personal financial statements

I would highlight two important segments of a business plan: **the mission statement** and **executive summary.** They are usually the first two items in a business plan about which some lenders and investors would want to talk to a business owner. Here is a sample of the mission statement and executive summary that were attached to a simple business plan that I had prepared for a client.

Lenders usually require that a business be in existence for about three years before they would consider lending money to the business. However, my client had a lot of confidence in her abilities, and she was able to discuss her business plan intelligently with a lender and obtained a line of credit for $40,000 to open her first store.

The mission statement

A business is formed to accomplish a mission or goal. The specific mission, goal, or purpose must be stated clearly. For example, to lend money, to provide lodging, to design clothing, to protect from child labor, to protect from violence against women, etc.

The mission statement must be designed to communicate to the company's managers, employees, lenders, customers or clients, and other stakeholders, the purpose, direction, and opportunity. A company should make adjustments to its mission statement when the mission statement has lost credibility or when it no longer defines a clear course or road map for the company.

A strong mission statement has three major characteristics:

1. **It focuses on specific goals.**
2. **It emphasizes the major policies and values that the company will honor. Include topics such as how the company will handle employees, customers, suppliers, distributors, stakeholders, and special interest groups.**
3. **It outlines and defines the competitive scope within which the company will operate, for example:**

   a. **The industry scope**
   b. **Market segment scope**
   c. **Competence scope**
   d. **Supply and product scope**
   e. **Geographical scope**

In order to clarify what I am talking about, here are three examples of mission statements:

1. **Here is a copy of the mission statement by Motorola for the technology company Motorola Corporation:** "The purpose of Motorola is to honorably serve the needs of the community by providing services and products of superior quality at a fair price to our customers so as to earn an adequate profit which is required for the total enterprise to grow and provide an opportunity for our employees and shareholders to achieve their reasonable personal objectives."
2. **Here is a copy of the mission statement of petroleum company Amoco:** "Amoco is a worldwide integrated petroleum and chemical company. We discover and develop petroleum resources and provide high quality products and services to our customers. We operate our business responsibly to achieve a high financial return; balanced with our long-term growth to benefit our shareholders and to fulfill our commitment to the community and the environment."

Write your business mission statement below

_____

_____

_____

_____

_____

_____

_____

_____

The executive summary must clearly state the exact amount of money that is required, the purpose of the loan, and give a detailed and clear explanation about what the loan will be used for and why it is needed. Here is a sample of the executive summary that was attached to a business plan I had prepared for a client. She was able to obtain a line of credit for $40,000 to open her first store.

Executive Summary

I graduated from high school and the Fashion Institute of Technology and interned and was trained by some of the best designers. I have done forty-five successful fashion shows, which provided me with 110 clients, including two major retail stores, plus the strong visibility that I have today. I worked for long hours in retail establishments helping customers and moving up the ranks to retailer manager and purchasing manager while I attended trade, fashion, and textile shows and business workshops. This was my way of transforming myself from an employee into a business owner—a lifelong dream. However, I realize that to fulfill that dream I need to borrow money.

Loan amount: $40,000.

Purpose: To start a women's clothing store, to modernize the store to match those of my competitors, and to appeal to the changing demographics of customers shopping in the area. I plan to use $18,000 of my money to renovate the store, and use the loan as follows:

1. $16,000 of the loan to purchase security cameras, merchandise, supplies, furniture, clothing racks, hangers, and mannequins, and to lease computers, printer, cash machine, and terminals supplies.
2. $6,000 will be used for marketing and promotional items.
3. $18,000 will be held in as contingency funds (preferably to pay operating expenses for the first nine months).

Location: Livingston Street, downtown Brooklyn.

Competitive edge: Neat aisles, clean store, just-in-time inventory, fashionable clothing, and excellent customer service. I and my family members will not be taking a salary from the business; therefore, my overhead expenses will be lower than my competitors. That allows me to give free shipping to customers who order online, plus eye-popping discounts on a few items to encourage customers to shop and increase online and in-store traffic.

I am able to make decisions prudently and quickly. I also have a good business attorney and accountant, and a business advisor who will keep me on track and help me grow the business.

I have never filed for bankruptcy, and there are no pending lawsuits against me or liens against my property.

<u>Write your executive summary here</u>

_____

_____

_____

_____

_____

_____

_____

_____

Execution of your plan must be your prime objective. Execution is the discipline to get things done. It is the opposite of procrastination. Every so often people would do a lot of research and planning, and then they would procrastinate. They have the information and the strategy laid out, but they are afraid to take action. Hence, they lost great opportunities to other people who were less prepared than they were.

Planning

Let us begin the business planning process.

1. Suppliers: Your success in business will depend on **how much you know about your industry, who would say they know you, and who would trust you.**

Trust is not easily earned in today's business environment. Your suppliers are the lifeblood of your business, and they have a lot of business connections. Paying your suppliers should be a priority. If you have a genuine problem with their products or services, work with them to solve the problem. Be ethical—don't try to rob, outfox, or hoodwink your suppliers and ruin a good relationship and a chance to grow your business. **"Don't be penny-wise and pound-foolish."** Behaving with honesty and integrity is sometimes an act of courage, but it is a priceless reward to safeguard your reputation.

2. Sales: Contact the **Small Business Expo** and find out when their networking event and trade show will be in New York State or fly to New York. The website address is www.TheSmallBusinessExpo.com, or you can Google the name.

Your salespeople must be able to sell your products or service to keep their jobs and keep you in business. Team fit is critical for starting and sustaining sales momentum. You must take advantage of every opportunity to sell your service or your products to prospective buyers. Selling is everything in this global economy. If your company designs and sells products, then you would be required to hire designers, technicians, and/or engineers. Everybody in you technology department should learn from people in your sales, marketing, and accounting departments how the innovations and products they will create need to be sold. Hence, innovation, costs, and selling price must blend nicely into your product to attract buyers.

I have seen many beautifully designed products get rejected by retail stores such as Walmart and Costco because the selling price of each product that was rejected was above the price the retailers would buy them and then make a reasonable profit. Don't lose faith in your products if they are rejected by superstores such as Walmart and Costco. Selling is full of rejections, and your faith in your business and products will constantly be tested. They may not buy your products, but other stores will be happy to take your products on consignment and sell them at a higher margin, so shop around your products and keep an open mind.

What do you plan to do if your sales are soaring or going through the roof? Some experts will tell you to expand your operations. If you are selling a product, some experts will tell you to open another store. If you are selling a service, some experts will tell you to open another office. They may tell you that customers are taking advantage of you and encourage you to raise prices. That appears be true, but that is what everybody will do —they will take advantage of a bargain. Sure, you may raise the price and gain additional revenue, but this is a risk that you must undertake with **caution and intelligence**. You must understand your customer base well enough to take that risk. Here is how some of us have approached that situation. However, you are free to approach this situation from a different angle.

In my consultation practice, I price my services so that my business will always be busy in peak times, good times, and bad times. I charge clients the same price in a good or a bad economy. When the economy is booming, clients are more than happy to pay in advance. It may seem to them that they are getting a bargain, but they are paying the same price in a recession, and they are not complaining because that is their price.

I learned this pricing system from working for clients in the merchant marine industry. Those clients must lease out their ships under long-term contracts, and the lessees must be able to negotiate freight at reasonable prices to keep those ships working in peak times and slow times.

3. Energy: High electricity and fuel costs can put your company's products at a disadvantage against imported products. Before you open your business, and during the time that you are doing your feasibility study (evaluating the cost and benefit of starting or buying a business), pay close attention to the cost of energy, and budget appropriately. In many countries, businesses that have failed have blamed the high cost of electricity as one of the primary reasons for their demise.

4. Business Valuation: Business valuation is the appraisal of the economic value of a business. **Who would need a business valuation report?** Buyers, partners, courts, taxing authorities, creditors, and investors would need it.

I appreciate feedback from my readers and clients. My e-mail address is **ClemBarry@ aol.com**, and my website is **www.ConsultantBarry.com**.

CHAPTER 15
BUSINESS BUDGETING

I am sure you have heard the proverbial sayings:

1. **"Money talks."**
2. **"Cash is king."**
3. **"Out of money, out of business."**

Many businesses have failed because:

1. **They focus too much on outpricing their competitors and lose sight of product quality and customer service.**
2. **They were undercapitalized (lack of adequate working capital).**
3. **They did not have a realistic business plan (a guide).**
4. **They refused to seek proper financial advice.**

A budget is an integral part of every business. It is a formal expression of the goals and plans of a business, and it requires a business owner to focus ahead of time and formalize future goals.

Most seasonal business owners get into trouble because of cash flow problems:

1. They are too lazy to write anything down—prepare a budget.
2. They think they are smart enough to keep numbers and details in their heads.
3. They pretend not to be interested in the reality of the situation. Usually they will pretend not to care. Oftentimes their responses would be: "I just don't want to know," or "Everything will work out fine."

A budget creates an early warning system that an owner or financial manager can use to evaluate business accomplishments and weaknesses and take appropriate actions quickly.

Failing to use a budget, especially a **cash budget** to help seasonal business owners predict a cash shortage before it occurs, a sudden decline in seasonal sales revenue, or customers who did not pay the business on time, would create a **"cash crunch"** that would impact negatively on the business's **cash flow** and **working capital,** and force the owners to borrow **emergency funds** at high interest rates or **file for bankruptcy.**

If the business has a budget, the owner or financial manager would be able to predict the cash shortage or deficit and make early arrangement for a **revolving line of credit** from the bank—**a contingency plan**. Lenders want to do business with people who are in control of the financial situations of a business—**people who are visionary**.

Here is a short list of some of the frequently used budgets. A wise business owner would take the time and have the patience to design each budget and allocate resources to operate and grow the business.

1. **Sales budget**
2. **Production (manufacturing) budget**
3. **Cash budget**
4. **Marketing budget**
5. **Capital expenditure budget**
6. **Operating budget**
7. **Administrative budget**
8. **Master (comprehensive) budget**

Sales budget: a sales budget is the key budget in the entire budgeting process, and **business owners should prepare this budget first**. It triggers a chain reaction that leads to the preparation and development of other budgets for your company. **The sales budget can be used to direct and control sales efforts by:**

1. **Product line**
2. **Customers**
3. **Territory**

4. Salesperson

After the sales budget is prepared, a decision can be made about the size of production that will be necessary or needed to meet the sales target. However, **the sales budget will usually require the preparation of a sales forecast** (prediction) to indicate how many orders and shipments the company will be required to make during the budget year. Hence, it is important that you **take into account the following three factors**:

1. **Your past experience**
2. **Economic and market trends**
3. **Your company's marketing policies and objectives**

1. **Your past experiences:** This pertains to the knowledge that you have acquired working in the industry. You may find the date that you need in past invoices or billing statements to customers in your filing cabinet or electronic database. The records will provide you with the following information:

   a. The date the product was sold
   b. The names of people who had bought your product or services
   c. Customers' addresses—location
   d. Customer's industry
   e. Salesperson's name
   f. The number of product sold (quantity sold).
   g. The unit price per product
   h. The total value of the order

Production (manufacturing) budget:

The production budget should be prepared after the sales budget is completed.

The production budget should be prepared after production planning and schedules of production activities are designed and established.

The production budget specifies the planned quantity of goods that is required to be manufactured during the budget period. This is usually comprised of the following:

1. **Established policies for maintaining the required inventory levels**
2. **The quantity of each product that is required to be manufactured during the budget period**
3. **Scheduling production activities by interim periods**

Cash budget: A cash budget is one of the most important budget forecasts in the operation of a business. **It is a projection of a company's cash inflow and outflow during a specific budget period. It shows how managers at the company planned to obtain cash and used or disbursed cash to pay expenses and expenditures during the budget period.**

The cash budget helps business owners and financial managers:

1. Avoid holding too much idle cash
2. Keep adequate cash balances in relation to the company's needs
3. Predict the cash requirement to operate and whether outside financing or funding will be required

There are two commonly used cash budget methods, both of which focus on the cash requirement of a company. They are the **cash receipt and disbursement,** and the **adjustment income** methods.

Preparing and using a budget

The budgeting process usually begins when the business owner or financial manager prepares a detailed analysis of estimated business income and expenses for the current year.

1. The company should adapt a flexible budgeting system, whereby every month the budgeted income and expenses are reviewed and compared to the actual income and expenses for that month. Doing that would reveal the actual shortage or surplus (variances) in the budget. The owner can focus on how much of the variances relate to sales volume and how much was due to operating inefficiencies—"normalizing the budget."

2. If the budgeted amounts exceed the actual amounts, then a negative variance exists. Adjustments to the budget, including tighter operations management and reduction in staff, may be necessary to maintain business solvency, and the owner or financial manager can be held accountable for neglecting to take immediate and decisive actions to prevent a recurrence of the results.

CHAPTER 16
STARTING A BUSINESS

"You are never too old to set another goal or dream a new dream."
—Les Brown

"The secret of getting ahead is getting started."
—Agatha Christie

"The journey of a thousand miles begins with a single step."
—Miyamoto Musashi

"You will never get there if you let the journey intimidate you."
—Stephen Mayer

"Credibility is important in business. Everything is based on trust."

"There are no guarantees … only opportunities."

Lenny Niemeyer, affectionately called the Brazilian Bikini Queen, saw an untapped niche in the apparel market. She started out dropping off, picking up, and checking on orders from customers living in the favelas, or slums. She modified store-bought bikinis in her garage and made bikinis for customers out of whatever materials she could obtain. After many years of selling her bikinis to established companies that put their labels on her pieces and reaped huge profits, Niemeyer developed the courage and opened her first store in the beachfront neighborhood of Ipanema. Today she employs about 180 seamstresses. She has a legion of VIP customers and owns twenty-six stores in Brazil, and several stores in the United Kingdom, France, the Bahamas, and the United States of America.

Risk is unavoidable

Sensible and calculated risks are the paths to success. You take a risk every time you try to do something new. Accepting your first job was a risk, and every time you got a promotion was also a risk. You could have failed and gotten fired because you had never done the job before, but you were resilient, and you took the challenge and responsibility seriously. You did not succumb to fear, and as a result you became successful. The same thing holds true for starting a business. If you have a business plan, and you have developed a business model and are willing to risk uncertainty and rejection, your business will become very successful.

If you are planning to start a business, and you feel isolated because your friends and family are not supportive of your plans and ideas, here are two quotes that will boost your spirit and motivate you to follow your dream and become successful:

"He who holds someone on the ground is also on the ground." —Proverb

"I am too positive to be doubtful, too optimistic to be fearful, and too determined to be defeated." —Clemson Barry

Why start a business?

You can start a business and have fun doing what you like and get paid for doing it while you build equity. There are people who are working at jobs that they don't like, and they are unhappy every day they go to work. Some people get laid off and can't find a job to help them pay their expenses.

AARP survey

Three out of every ten self-employed workers older than age forty-five turned to entrepreneurship after they were laid off, according to a new AARP survey. The findings suggest that starting a business is a good way for older workers to bounce back. Seventy-two percent of older entrepreneurs said their businesses are profitable.

When should you start?

"Better three hours too soon than one minute too late." —Proverb

Some people have said the best time to start a business is in a strong or recovering economy. However, after taking a close look at business registration data in every state in the United States of America and some EU member states, I would say with absolute certainty that there is no special time to start a business. The data have shown that new businesses have been launched during **economic recessions**, during **economic recovery**, and during **economic boom**. New York State launched over fifty thousand new businesses in 2012, the toughest year since the worldwide economic recession started in 1997. **http://www.bighappenshere.com.**

Many businesses launched in the middle of the economic recession are still operating today. The secret that is responsible for those businesses being able to survive during the economic recession is a strong and realistic business plan that was skillfully executed in a timely manner, and then analyzed for results and modified.

Where should you start?

Prioritize. Prepare a list of three things that you must get done today. Start by putting your personal finances in order. It is imperative that you organize your personal finances before you start or buy a business, or buy a franchise. Lenders and investors respect visionary borrowers who have organized their personal finances before approaching them. (Please read the chapter: **"Personal financial planning."**)

You can choose to differentiate your business or blend in with the crowd. If you choose to differentiate your business, then you should start by working diligently to make your business unique and distinctive from the competition. Here is my reason. If customers cannot differentiate between your business and those of your successful competitors, then why would they choose to shop at your businesses instead of shopping at your competitors' businesses?

How should you start?

Find something that you enjoy and excel in that other people don't like to do. People will always pay someone else to do what they don't like doing.

List those things that you are passionate about and which come to you naturally. Offer something that is innovative and valuable to your target market or customers—something that would create a huge demand and differentiate you in the marketplace. **Here are two ways to proceed:**

1. You have solved a personal problem or a problem you have at home or on your job, and you realized there are many people who have that problem and would be happy to find a solution.

"I could not find the right product, and I realized many people had the same problem that I had, so I created a product."

—Liza Price, founder, cosmetic firm Carols Daughter

—Mary Kay Ash, founder, cosmetic firm Mary Kay

—Dr. Rodan and Dr. Fields, founders, Proactiv Solution

2. Examine a product or service that you like, and find a way to make it simpler, faster, or better. "We don't make most of the things that you use; we make most of the things you use better." —BASF Corp.

"Respect doesn't come from the kind of work you do; it comes from the way you do the work." —Kenneth L. Shipley

Everybody cannot do the same job because talents and aspirations vary. If everybody does the same job, economic growth would stagnate, and many of us would not be alive. Hence, vibrant economic activities and economic growth can only come from a diverse labor force that is comprised of people in different trades and professions. I call that **"economic empowerment."**

Success Stories

Furniture restoration

When Roger attended college, he also worked on weekends doing furniture restoration with a friend. Roger graduated from college during the economic recession in 2010 and couldn't find a job. He was heartbroken, but he was courageous. He realized people were facing financial constraints, and they were not buying new furniture, so he printed some flyers offering to repair or restore their used furniture. He distributed the flyers door to door and met with the customers. He collected 50 percent down payment and took the furniture to his apartment and repaired it. Whenever he delivered the restored furniture, his customers inspected it in his van, which was parked outside their homes, and paid him before he brought the furniture inside their homes. Business was booming, and Roger rented a storefront and hired three assistants. Roger's attention to details and innovation has made his shop the ultimate destination for furniture restoration, upholstery work for cars and bikes, new furniture, and kitchen cabinets.

Service technician

Jenny was a sales manager for a major consumer products manufacturer. Her husband, Tom, was a technician for a technology company that sells and services office equipment. The couple has two children, ages two and four.

Jenny was concerned that Tom would get laid off because his employer was constantly downsizing the company, so she encouraged him to start a company and quit his employer.

Tom and Jenny prepared a business plan and rented office space in a low-rent area. Jenny printed and mailed flyers and brochures about the company's services to her business contacts while Tom distributed flyers and brochures to people with home offices and businesses in the community.

In the beginning, business activity was slow, and Tom handled all the service calls by himself. His price was 35 percent lower than his competitors'. He gave customers a warranty, and he was available to work 24/7. Customers were satisfied with the service, and they referred other customers to him. He subsequently hired two technicians to help him with the workload.

Jenny quit her job two years later and joined Tom. She was tired of constantly traveling and spending time away from the children, including holidays and birthdays. She became the sales manager for the company, and she hired and trained several sales associates to help her generate more business for the company.

One year later, the couple bought a building and moved the business to a new location. Jenny and Tom became the exclusive agents for a major electronics manufacturer, and they won bids and contracts to sell and service office equipment and supplies to large companies and the government; and they are on schedule to pay off the mortgage on their building in five years. They work during the week and take weekends off. Weekend calls and after-hours service calls during the week are taken by an answering service company and routed to their on-call technicians.

Jenny and Tom have plans to diversify into other businesses.

Many people have started their businesses in their basement, garages, college dorm rooms, or kitchens, and they have become very successful.

- **Liza Price**, CEO of the cosmetic firm Carols Daughter, started out from her kitchen while she kept her full-time job in Manhattan.
- **Bill Gates**, the founder of Microsoft, and his friend Paul Allen developed and launched their computer software and revolutionized the software industry.
- **Richard Branson** started out his Virgin brand as a student magazine in school and later as a record company in his basement and by selling his records on the sidewalk.
- **Michael Dell**, the founder of Dell computers, started selling IBM personal computers from his bedroom in college.
- **Mary Kay Ash,** the founder of the famous cosmetic line Mary Kay, started out hawking her product from door to door.
- **Colonel Sanders,** the founder of KFC, started out cooking and selling fried chicken from the back of his car.

- **Frederick Smith**, founder of FedEx, dreamed about owning a delivery company, so he wrote a term paper for his professor about the kind of business he envisioned, and the rest is history.
- **Shawn Fanning** started Napster to create and share music with his friends. Napster has changed the way music is sold and consumed, and it has revolutionized the music industry.
- **Seth Berkowitz** baked cookies to eat during late-night studies in his college dorm room. Word spread and **Insomnia Cookies** was born. It became a hit with college students and the local news, and the rest is history.
- **Other first-generation entrepreneurs** who have started out small and have made their microenterprises **"the next big thing"** are: Mark Zuckerberg, Suze Orman, Martha Stewart, Oprah Winfrey, Richard Simmons, Warren Buffett, Steve Jobs, Howard Schultz, Sam Walton, Larry Ellison, Charles Schwab, Ralph Lauren, Rupert Murdoch, Jeff Bezos, Larry Page, Eric Schmidt, etc.

Questions

How would you know what business you should start?

Answer

Anybody who wants to own a business should define the kind of business that he or she would be happy to own, and get some hands-on experience by working in that industry. That person should write a business plan about how he or she envisioned the business and how the plan will be executed. This individual must be prepared to seize the opportunity when it arises and be persistent. Opportunities are lost because of the lack of preparation, procrastination, and pessimism.

What is your biggest challenge or concern about starting a business or being a business owner? Why?

_____

_____

_____

If you could have one question answered about starting or growing your business, what would the question be? Why?

_____

_____

_____

Why did some businesses fail?

1. **The owners and their businesses were incompatible**, and they quickly lost focus about their business's mission.
2. **The owners were sued** by established competitors for breach of trademark and copyright laws. The cost of defending themselves and their products drained their finances and left them broke.
3. **The business was devoid of new ideas, innovation, and hands-on leadership**. The owners were lackadaisical. They sat back and gave their employees free rein to run the business. The owners surrounded themselves with people who would always agree with their belief and strategy—**yes men and yes women** who would tell them what they wanted to hear even when their attitude or perception was detrimental to the business.
4. **The government shut them down** because they didn't comply with employment rules and tax regulations.
5. **They had taken their customers for granted**. They failed to maintain the quality or value of the product and service that their customers had become accustomed to receiving. Hence, their product and service were bypassed or overlooked in favor of those from competitors—**social backlash**.
6. **They had failed to modify or change their business model** to suit the changes in the demographics of the population and the changes in economic and market trends or conditions.
7. **They had poor or bad financial and business management**.
8. **List your experience or belief why a business with which you were familiar had failed.**

_____

_____

_____

Take this challenge

1. Sports bar and lounge

"For every failure, there's an alternative course of action. You just have to find it. When you come to a roadblock, take a detour."
—Mary Kay Ash

Karl borrowed money from his pension and opened a twenty-five hundred-square-foot **sports bar and lounge** in a city with a population of 105,000, with median income averaging $60,000 and 45 percent of the population between the ages of twenty and thirty-five. To cater to the "hip" crowd, he planned on hiring a DJ and having live karaoke.

He hired a carpenter to soundproof the ceiling to stop the noise from distracting the tenants who were living above the bar. The Sanitation Department inspected and approved the kitchen, storage areas, bathroom, and other facilities. The Fire Department inspected the premises. It met the city building code, and Karl received a permit for the maximum number of occupants allowed in his premises. The city granted him a permit and a beer license. The community board approved his liquor license application after meeting with the neighboring church, school, and community groups and inspecting the bar and lounge.

His consultant told him that every bar must maintain at least 80 percent of its customers and bring in at least 20 percent new customers annually in order to maintain profitability. He knows he has to keep coming up with new things to keep patrons coming back, and he is aware that the more women frequent his club the more men would be interested in patronizing his club, so he made the club safe and appealing to women.

He hired an experienced DJ to set up the music equipment and stage lighting, and experienced bartenders and waiters to set up the bar, VIP lounge, TV, pool/billiards area, and bar lighting, because the décor and location of the liquor bottles and beer tap can encourage patrons to extend their stay. The longer they stay at the bar, the more they would buy, thus increasing sales and profits.

He wanted the business to be known as a safe place, where patrons could relax and enjoy his signature food and drinks, and businesspeople could use as an informal meeting place to discuss business out of the office, so he hired a top chef to design new recipes, make fresh delicious food and beverages, and train his cooks. He and his staff taste and critique the food and drinks.

He hired an experience bartender (master mixologist) to train his bartenders how to properly mix the new drinks and avoid overpouring and spillage. To avoid **skimming from the top**, Karl installed a state of the art system whereby he would know **the size of the drop**—how much money each bartender must turn over at the end of his/her shift without alerting the bartenders that the bookkeeper is aware of their actions/honesty. The training and the system have saved his business thousands of dollars in profits.

The food and drinks were a major hit with the customers, and business was brisk for five consecutive years. Karl neglected the business for a while by practicing hands-off or absentee ownership. A lot of new bars began opening in the neighborhood and luring customers away from his bar. His business was hurt by competitive intrusion, and monthly sales went from $65,000 to $43,000. He was losing $22,000 per month, or $5,500 weekly, while monthly overhead expenses increased to $35,000.

Bartenders were earning fewer tips, and they were working longer hours, so they retaliated by giving their customers free drinks **(overpouring)** in exchange for bigger tips. Bar sales fell to $450 per night while bar costs rose to $800 per night. The business had survived the competition because it is operating in a strong market; but its days are numbered. It would not be able to survive for long without effective leadership and direction.

Karl hired a mystery shopper (undercover customer) who told him what was happening at his business. He wants to turn around or reform the business and make it profitable. If you were Karl, how would you revive the business? What would you do differently?

_____

_____

_____

_____

How did some people outperform their competitors?

1. **They clearly defined and communicated their brand, business model, and product or service to the public**.

2. **They set realistic goals**, with a focus on quality products, service and sales, etc. They were focused, motivated, and determined to become successful. Contact the Small Business Expo and find out when its networking event and trade show will be in York State, or fly to New York. The website address is **www. TheSmallBusinessExpo.com**, or you can Google the name.

3. **They had a strategy to achieve their goals**—work smarter, not harder.

4. **They had allocated the necessary resources**—finance, labor, marketing, etc.

5. **They executed their plans in a timely manner**—timing is everything.

6. **They monitored and modified the results**—resilient and results-oriented.

7. **They were not afraid to think outside the box** and used unconventional, noncontroversial tactics to achieve their goals—practical brilliance.

8. **They had maintained a strong cash reserve** while they focused primarily on existing markets, and they did not miss an opportunity to expand operations or to acquire a competitor or a company that complemented their line of products or services—organic growth and growth through acquisition.

9. **List your experiences here**_____

_____

_____

_____

_____

I appreciate feedback from my readers and clients. My e-mail address is **ClemBarry@ aol.com**, and my website is **www.ConsultantBarry.com**.

CHAPTER 17
MICROENTERPRISES

"You are never too old to set another goal or dream a new dream."
—Les Brown

I am sure you have heard the proverbial sayings:

1. **"Nothing ventured, nothing gained."**
2. **"Your attitude will determine your altitude."**

Every person should explore, learn, and always be ready to take action—take reasonable risks (a leap of faith) and be persistent. An opportunity may present itself, or you will have to create your own opportunity.

"What would life be like if we had no courage to attempt anything?"
—Vincent Van Gogh

Where should you start?

Many of the large corporations that exist today were once microenterprises. (Also read the chapter **"Starting a Business."**) They were started in the founder's:

1. Basements
2. Garages
3. Kitchen
4. Spare bedroom
5. College dormitory (dorm room)

6. Street sidewalks
7. Back of a vehicle

Lenny Niemeyer, affectionately called the Brazilian Bikini Queen, saw an untapped niche in the apparel market. She started out dropping off, picking up, and checking on orders from customers living in the favelas, or slums. She modified store-bought bikinis in her garage and made bikinis for customers out of whatever materials she could get her hands on. After many years of selling her bikinis to established companies that put their labels on her pieces and reaped huge profits, Niemeyer developed the courage and opened her first store in the beachfront neighborhood of Ipanema. She employs 180 seamstresses, owns twenty-six stores in Brazil and several stores in the United Kingdom, France, the Bahamas and the United States of America.

Microenterprises are usually started by people who want to work but could not find a job or by college students using their dorm rooms as small business incubators. They are also started by people who are currently employed and who are using their hobbies to supplement their incomes. They are also started by people who want something to fall back on if they are fired from their jobs unexpectedly, and by people who are preparing to quit their jobs someday and work full time in their own business and leave the business for future generations. This kind of business incubator (working from home) is the cheapest way to start a business, test ideas, and get feedback from customers, family, and friends before investing more money to produce a product or service and venturing out to pay rent and other operations expenses for an office or storefront.

Another positive reason to operate a microenterprise from your home is you will be able to deduct business expenses on your business or personal tax return for operating an office at home." This is an ideal way to open an office at home or start a business at home if you are a contractor, a paralegal, or are selling products online, or if you like designing and hosting websites, preparing tax returns, selling real estate, selling insurance policies, baking cakes and cookies, decorating, or catering to weddings and private parties, etc.

The downside to operating from home is you must be disciplined to set priorities and accomplish goals. If you are the kind of person who likes to chitchat, then working from your home in isolation of support staff to constantly talk to can be rough on you. Also, as a solo person you must be hands-on and be diversified, as oftentimes you would have to do everything by yourself if you cannot afford to hire employees.

When should you start?

There is no special time to start a new business. Data from several states in the United States of America and EU member states have shown that new businesses have been launched during **economic recessions**, **economic recoveries**, and **economic booms**. During the worldwide economic recession that started in 2007, over thirty thousand new businesses were launched annually in New York State. The result is similar and slightly lower in other US and EU member states. SMEs in the European Union represent 98 percent of all enterprises, or twenty-three million firms, and employ 85 percent, or eighty-seven million employees, in the EU. **www.BigHappensHere.com**

How should you start?

1. You must be selective about what you want to accomplish. First, you should Identify and focus on your strengths and passion. A combination of both elements would enable you to quickly identify and capitalize on opportunities that would make you successful.
2. Offer something that is needed in your market, and price it to increase demand. (Look closely at the competition to see how you can differentiate your business and create or increase demand for your products and services.)
3. Be specific about what you want to achieve, including the size of the business you want to build. Have a written plan and a strategy and be prepared to execute your plan and strategy quickly and make adjustments as you proceed.
4. Competitors are not buying your products and services, so don't waste your time thinking about them. Give only 2 percent of your attention to the competition in order to keep up with changes in the marketplace and in your industry. Please remember, you are not operating in a vacuum.
5. Customers are buying your products and services, so focus on your customers and give 98 percent of your attention to customer feedback and customer service, and learn everything that you can about your customers, including but

not limited to: customers' needs, wants, preferences, buying patterns, incomes, wealth, birthdays, anniversaries, etc.

Here is an e-mail that I received when I was writing the manuscript for this book.

Hi, Clem: I want to open a woman's clothing store, but I do not have experience selling clothing, and I do not have a lot of money to invest. I have excellent credit and a credit card with $2,500 available credit that I can use. What do you recommend? Thanks, **Cassie.**

Hi, Cassie: One of the reasons why new businesses (start-ups) failed is because the founders were not knowledgeable about operating the business, or the founders and the businesses were not compatible. The founders had invested money into businesses without first getting hands-on training and experience and understanding the nature of the businesses and what it takes to become successful in business and in a particular industry.

Here is my advice

Prepare yourself

Take a part-time job in a clothing store for one month and experience its operation and see if what you experience on the job meets your expectations. Are you happy to go to work there every day? Are you good at multitasking; that is, do you like wearing many hats?

Attend trade shows

While you are working there, attend trade shows and meet with clothing suppliers. At those trade shows you will notice that suppliers promote more than their companies and products. They promote a career, success, lifestyle, confidence, and trust. They promote to salespeople and prospective customers qualities that make their products and companies appealing or stand out in the industry.

Meet with suppliers

1. Find out from those suppliers their terms and conditions for supplying you with clothing. You said you don't have money to buy clothing (inventory), so ask those suppliers if they would give you clothing on consignment. Therefore, you would pay for what you sell and would return to them what you did not sell.

2. If they insist that you must give them an initial down payment, then use your credit card to make your first payment. If you have a job, you can save some money every pay period until you have the full down payment. If you do not have a credit card or a job, then ask your close friends and family for help. You can become innovative and raise money from prospective customers. This is called crowd-funding, and you can get details on the website KickStarter.com

3. Contact the **Small Business Expo** and find out when their networking event and trade show will be in York State, or fly to New York. The website address is **TheSmallBusinessExpo.com**; or you can Google the name. At the Small Business Expo, you are putting you products or services in front of your prospective customers or clients. You are meeting face to face with your target customers. If you need more detail, visit my website, **ConsultantBarry.com,** and click on the link "Starting a Business."

Starting your business

1. Form a corporation or LLC (incorporate the business with your state or country).
2. Set your goals (have a strategic/long-term plan).
3. Start selling your clothing from home so that you are spending less on overhead expenses. Hence, your clothing prices should be able to fit the budgets of a lot of prospective buyers.

Financing your business

(Read the chapter "Raising Capital.")

Marketing your business

Publicity is not easy to obtain, so make your pitch to close friends and family members, and use your online connections (social media network) to make regular weekly pitches. Here is what you should do:

1. Visualize your goal.
2. First impression means everything.
3. Be persistent.
4. Look for and capitalize on hidden opportunities.
5. Focus on your strengths.
6. Hire qualified people to handle what you are not qualified or comfortable doing.

Suppliers are looking for motivated retailers or vendors just like you to help them grow their businesses. Your No. 1 job as a small-business owner is to sell. Your job is to motivate, inspire, and convince customers, potential investors, and family members that your business idea is worthwhile. It typically requires passion for your project, a coherent message, and, most importantly, a confident delivery of that message. Other tactics are considered time-wasting approaches, and they will produce little or no results.

Be ethical

Don't try to rob, outfox, or hoodwink your suppliers and ruin a good relationship and a chance to grow your business. Behaving with honesty and integrity is sometimes an act of courage; but it is a priceless reward to safeguard your reputation.

Success Stories

"The secret of getting ahead is getting started."
—Agatha Christie

Anybody can start a business and become successful. Find something that you are passionate about, have a plan to make it work, and a long-term strategy to make it become successful. Find a way to market your passion and continue to modify you plan to meet customers' needs and changes in the economy.

Hair accessory

Many home-based businesses and microenterprises have become successful companies by outsourcing work to outside companies and manufacturers that were able to provide them with quality work at low labor cost. Tomima Edmark, the inventor of **"TopsyTail,"** a French-style hair accessory for women and girls, started her company, TopsyTail Corporation, in 1991. A skillful saleswoman, she marketed her product to department stores and fashion magazines. For her business acumen and inventive skills, she received many invitations and appeared in *Forbes Magazine*, on *Good Morning America* and on *The Oprah Winfrey Show*. Sales of her product grew to $100 million in 1992. What is interesting about her success is that instead of hiring thirty or more employees, Tomima and two workers established a network of twenty vendors and outsourced everything to them, from product manufacturing to servicing the department store accounts. However, she was smart enough to kept control of the marketing strategies and new product development, the core competencies of her company.

Fashion designer

Paul Smith, the UK fashion designer and owner of fashion labels and retail stores Paul Smith, opened his first store at age twenty-four. He used his savings of 600 pounds (approximately US $810) to open a small twelve-foot-by-twelve-foot store because the bank had refused to loan him money. Several years later, and with lots of determination, he had managed to secure a licensing agreement that paid him a small annual royalty of $15,000. That small but steady income stream had helped him pay the operating costs, avoid borrowing money, and build his business and brand slowly and prudently. The business is debt free and the current income stream comes from his retail shops, wholesaling, freelance, and consulting.

Dog training and boarding

Three years ago, the company Paul worked for laid him off after eighteen years of service. He has always had a passion for training dogs, so getting laid off was a blessing in disguise. He studied and received his dog training and behavioral consulting certificate. He cleaned out and soundproofed his garage and used his severance pay to convert it into a kennel, training area, and boarding area. He walks the dogs, caters to their special diets, and keeps their owners apprised through Skype. The fee for training the dogs varies. However, the fee for boarding and supervised care of the dogs can range from $15 to $60 per night, plus a 15 percent service fee. The business was profitable in the first year and has been every year thereafter.

Internet cafe

John opened an **Internet cafe with a bakery** after he was laid off from his job. He had been planning for two years to own his business. He was trained as a local agent to sell products and repair mobile phones exclusively for a telecommunications company. He also designed websites and repaired equipment and computers for customers. The business was profitable in three months, and he expanded the menu to include breakfast and lunch. His shop is always filled with energy and is abuzz with young people studying, and everyone eating, drinking coffee, or just having a conversation.

I appreciate feedback from my readers and clients. My e-mail address is **ClemBarry@ aol.com**, and my website is **www.ConsultantBarry.com**.

CHAPTER 18
ENTREPRENEURSHIP

Entrepreneurship in the United States of America is similar to SMEs in the European Union, Africa, and Asia. The business and accounting terminologies may be different, but the concept, principles and methods of operations are similar. Business owners in the United States of America are market oriented or market savvy. They are very competitive and aggressive. If your business becomes complacent, it will lose market share quickly to competitors with aggressive marketing techniques.

USA versus EU

In the United Kingdom and some European countries, employers or business owners must deduct payroll taxes from their employees' wages. In addition, they are subject to collect value added tax (VAT) for selling products and services. **Those countries use the PAYE system to make payroll deductions:**

1. Income tax
2. National Insurance Scheme (NIS)
3. National Housing Scheme (NHS)
4. National Education Scheme/Fund (NES/NEF)

**In the United Kingdom, payroll taxes are reported immediately.

** In some European countries, the process is slow, and a new business must encounter a lot of red tape and hurdles. Hence, it can take up to three years to get a business permit and license approved.

In the United States of America, employers must:

In the United States of America, employers or business owners must deduct payroll taxes from their employees' wages. In addition they are subject to collect sales tax for selling products and services. Some services are exempt from sales tax.

The United States of America uses the PAYE system to make payroll deductions:

1. Federal and state income taxes
2. Social Security and Medicare taxes
3. Unemployment and workers' compensation taxes

** In the United States of America, payroll taxes are reported quarterly.

**In the United States of America, the process is quick, and a business can be incorporated in one day, and most business licenses (except alcohol and tobacco licenses) can take up to thirty days.

Thousands of medium-size and large businesses that we admire today have started out as **microenterprises** in a kitchen, basement, bedroom, or garage. They have come a long way from where they started many years ago to where they are today.

Risk is unavoidable

Sensible and calculated risks are the paths to success. You take a risk every time you try to do something new. Accepting your first job was a risk, and every time you got a promotion was also a risk. You could have failed and gotten fired because you had never done the job before, but you were resilient and took the challenge and responsibility seriously. You did not succumb to fear, and as a result you became successful. The same thing is true for starting any business. If you have a plan, and you are willing to risk uncertainty and rejection, your business will become very successful.

Do you have what it takes to become a successful entrepreneur?

There is a bit of entrepreneurship in all of us. I have known small farmers who have improvised watering systems to bring water to their animals and to water their crops during periods of drought. I have watched a documentary about people who improvised a watering system to distill moonshine whisky in the forest, miles away from the river. Those are forms of entrepreneurships because they involve innovation that lifts people out of poverty.

Here is how some of my connections on LinkedIn have described entrepreneurship:

1. "Being an entrepreneur means you're an optimist, plain and simple. You have the belief, courage, commitment, passion, and plan to act on your vision. You are a player in the game of capitalism, not a spectator, whether your idea is brand new, or it is a twist from an original idea.
   —Barry, M (owner, personal training company)

2. "Entrepreneurs identify areas that are underperforming and are ripe for disruption. They go in, shake up the market, and increase productivity."
   —Richard Branson (Virgin Companies)

My mission is to give you insights into the fascinating world of entrepreneurship, to challenge you and keep you inspired, to help you see the opportunities in every challenge, and to motivate you as you continue to grow your business, fulfill the vision and dream that you are passionate about, and make a name for yourself.

Transition from microenterprise to entrepreneurship

Entrepreneurship is the driving force in every modern economy. People's willingness to start new businesses and leverage their successes have created new jobs, reduced unemployment, and produced vibrant economies around the world. Thousands of businesses that we admire today started out as **microenterprises**, and they have grown to the size they are today.

An entrepreneur has to have natural qualities in addition to those that he or she has developed. Not every entrepreneur may want to grow a large business. Some entrepreneurs may prefer to remain small or medium—small and medium enterprises (SMEs). That is okay because the choice they have made or will make should be a personal and comfortable choice that every entrepreneur is free to make.

Your responsibilities as an entrepreneur would increase dramatically from what you were accustomed to when you were operating as a microenterprise. A successful entrepreneur must be a supporter of growth during good and bad economic times and must be prepared to become more innovative and creative while maintaining the quality and consistency of products and services.

When the economy is strong, new opportunities are always available to replace those opportunities that were lost. Hence, in a strong economy, entrepreneurs will focus more on pushing the business to generate more income, and they will focus less on operating the business efficiently. When the economy changes, and times are tough and opportunities become scarce and survival of the fittest has become the norm, those entrepreneurs become desperate and do desperate things.

1. They scramble to obtain new income streams, so they cut back on staff and services in the hope of outlasting their weaker competitors.
2. They become very aggressive and use the opportunity to take business away from their competitors in order to survive the economic recession.
3. They continue to do what they have been doing in a strong economy and hope to achieve the same result in a weak economy in spite of the changes in the economic and business environments.

So what are the traits of a successful entrepreneur? I have been an entrepreneur for over thirty years, and I have built my business from the ground up on a shoestring budget. Here is a summary of my advice:

1. Do not allow your ego to get in the way. Know your strengths and weaknesses, and work in tandem with your employees, suppliers, creditors, and customers/ clients (stakeholders), and continue to listen to them; get feedback from them, express your appreciation, and make appropriate and necessary adjustments.

2. Focus on the strengths of the unique products and services that the business provides, and manage your working capital skillfully. Spend money on things that would generate profits or a return on your investment.

3. Train yourself to look for ways to improve creativity, and encourage your team to find ways to provide products and services faster, better, cheaper, and easier.

4. Plan consistently and operate the business efficiently in good times so that it will survive and thrive in bad times.

5. You need to find the opportunities that will work for your business. Find out where the new opportunities are, or where they will come from, and plan how you and your business would capitalize on them and generate profit from them.

The time for strategic thinking and for implementing your strategic plans is now. Successful entrepreneurs are known for spotting opportunities more quickly than their competitors, looking at those opportunities objectively, and implementing their plans skillfully and in a timely manner. Here are some questions that you may want to ask yourself when you have spotted an opportunity:

1. Is this a good opportunity for me and my business?
2. Is that something to which I would want my business attached?
3. Will this opportunity help me and my business reach the goal that I have planned to accomplished?
4. Does my business have the resources that would enable it to capitalize on this opportunity?
5. Can my staff develop the skills that are necessary to capitalize on this opportunity, or could we outsource the work profitably?
6. If we don't have those skills, how long will it take us to develop those skills?
7. What impact will this opportunity have on my life and on my family?

Here are examples of some of the successful entrepreneurs in this book, *Sweet Success*:

Special event planning

Jo-Ann plans parties for "A" list clients. Some of those parties are hosted at her clients' estates, and sometimes she hosts parties at a facility that she owns.

John, a DJ and the owner of a bar, heard about her and hired her regularly to plan and host parties for him at her facility. He listened to her advice, and he knew how she set prices and implemented strategies to obtain clients. The business relationship was profitable, and whenever Jo-Ann held birthday, wedding, and Christmas parties for her clients, she would hire John as the DJ.

Soon Jo-Ann's clients were bypassing her and calling on John directly to DJ parties for them. He in turn hires and pays two of his friends to accompany him. One of his friends owns a landscaping company, and John pays him to groom the lawn and garden where the parties are held. The other friend owns a cleaning company, and John pays him to clean up at the end of the party.

John gives Jo-Ann's clients a package deal for the three services. The price tag was always a little above the price that Jo-Ann was charging just to plan the party. Jo-Ann lost several clients to John, and she accused him of backstabbing her. If you were Jo-Ann, what would be your strategy to keep your present clients, gain new clients, and regain former clients from John?

NOTES

_____
_____
_____
_____
_____
_____
_____
_____
_____
_____
_____
_____
_____

Clothing design and production

Sara Blakely is the sole owner of SpandX, a privately owned undergarment company that she started in her apartment in Decatur, **Georgia, USA**. She had built her company from a one-product business to a household name. From the beginning, she used whatever small savings she had, and she invested the profits into the business.

She spent money on things that make money. Hence, Sara did not spend a penny on traditional advertising; instead, she traveled from city to city selling her product, meeting with store owners, and encouraging her women customers to refer other women to her. Later she hawked her product on QVC, a television home shopping show. She did not receive help from a husband or an inheritance. The company is debt free. The company's estimated net profit, according to several analysts, is about $250 million. According to Forbes, the company is valued at about $1 billion. At age forty-one, Sara Blakely is reportedly the youngest woman to join the 2013 *Forbes* World's Billionaires list.

Clothing store

After you have finished reading the success story above, take the challenge below. Janice attended college to study business. During her time as a student, she worked part time when school was in session and full time during the summer and spring breaks for a large department store. After graduation from college, she continued working there, and she attended and participated in several trade shows. She acquired a love for fashion, and she attended and graduated from the Fashion Institute.

Three years later, she started sewing her clothing line at home while she kept her full-time job with the department store. On Sundays, she would showcase and sell her clothing from a booth that she rented in the local mall. She attended and won several fashion competitions, and she had a roster of clients, designers, and purchasing managers that were eager to do business with her.

Business was booming, and customer traffic became too heavy for her to do business at home and have a private life, so she withdrew all the money from her savings account and borrowed some money from relatives and friends and leased, renovated, and moved her business into a neighboring storefront.

The business was not in an ideal location that commanded heavy foot traffic; but it had a beautiful and professionally designed website that showcased the clothing line; and customers were able to buy clothing online and pay with credit cards, debit cards, and checks. She hired a full-time employee to work in the store while she kept her full-time job, and she took time off from work and spent that time and Sundays in her shop. The business was doing very well during the first nine months, so she quit her full-time job to devote more time to the business.

Her timing was bad. The country fell into an economic recession, and business became slow for every business owner on her block. She offered discount prices to encourage her regular customers to buy her clothing online, but they too were facing financial difficulties. Six months later, the business was barely breaking even, and she had difficulties paying the bills on time. She did not develop a cash budget or cash flow statement that would have warned her of the impending risks. Soon she ran out of savings, and she did not have a job whereby she could collect a paycheck.

Janice has acknowledged her mistakes, and she is aware that many people in other industries have made similar mistakes, and they have bounced back or recovered better than they were before the occurrence. She has also acknowledged that the business is undergoing a daily struggle to survive, but she is confident that it could weather the storm. She is resilient, and she is looking forward to better days. She is searching for a full-time night job whereby she would be able to work in her shop during the day.

Some people who are reading this story would say Janice was smart enough to start a business and have it operating for close to one year; therefore, she should be smart enough to turn around the negative results into a story about her triumph and inspiration. However, we all know that this is easier said than done.

Time is of the essence, and Janice is your sister or daughter and you want to help her rectify the problem and make the business profitable.

Hint: You do not want to disappoint, Janice so you are determined to find out how Janice's competitors are doing. You have decided to visit their stores as a mystery shopper and experience for yourself why customers do business with them and what their strengths and weaknesses are in the industry. Use the format below to prepare your survey report.

Point of Purchase Analysis

1. **Store layout and ease of location selection**

   _____

   _____

2. **Store cleanliness**

   _____

   _____

3. **Depth of product selection (product lines)**

   _____

   _____

4. **Employees' appearance**

   _____

   _____

5. **Employees' approach (work ethic)**

   _____

   _____

6. **Employees' knowledge of products**

   _____

   _____

7. **Advice on or about customer care**

   _____

   _____

8. **Product(s) recommendations (outside brands and store brand)**

   _____

   _____

9. **After-sale service program (warranty and return policy)**

   _____

   _____

10. Cash and wrap area appearance

_____

_____

11. General/overall service level

_____

_____

12. Telephone surveys

_____

_____

13. Market research projects undertaken

_____

_____

14. Exit polls

_____

_____

15. Customer service audits

_____

_____

Using the information on your survey report, how do you plan to solve the problem and turn the business around?

_____

_____

What time frame are we looking at? How long will it take you to produce results? Why?

_____

_____

I appreciate feedback from my readers and clients. My e-mail address is **ClemBarry@ aol.com**, and my website is **www.ConsultantBarry.com**.

CHAPTER 19
SMES

SMEs is the European Union's acronym or abbreviation for small and medium enterprises. The acronym is also used in Africa, Asia, and countries that have a business or financial relationship with the European Union. Accounting and business terminologies used in SMEs may be different from those used in entrepreneurships in the United States of America, but the concepts, principles, and methods of operation of both entities are similar. Business owners in the United States of America are market oriented or market savvy. They are very competitive and aggressive. If your business becomes complacent, it will lose market share quickly to competitors with aggressive marketing techniques.

USA versus EU

In the United Kingdom and some European countries, employers or business owners must deduct payroll taxes from their employees' wages. In addition, they are subject to collect value added tax (VAT) for selling products and services. **Those countries use the PAYE system to make payroll deductions:**

1. Income tax
2. National Insurance Scheme (NIS/NIC)
3. National Housing Scheme (NHS)
4. National Education Scheme/Fund (NES/NEF)

**In the United Kingdom, payroll taxes are reported immediately.

** In some European countries the process is slow, and a new business must encounter a lot of red tape and hurdles. Hence, it can take up to three years to get a business permit and license approved.

USA employers

In the United States of America, employers or business owners must deduct payroll taxes from their employees' wages. In addition, they are subject to collect sales tax for selling products and services. Some services are exempt from sales tax.

The United States of America uses the PAYE system to make payroll deductions:

1. Federal and state income taxes
2. Social Security and Medicare taxes
3. Unemployment and workers' compensation tax

** In the United States of America, payroll taxes are reported quarterly.

**In the United States of America the process is quick, and a business can be incorporated in one day, and most business licenses (except alcohol and tobacco licenses) can take up to thirty days.

Two main factors determine whether a company is an SME:

1. **The number of employees**
2.**Either turnover or balance sheet total**

Company category	Employees	Turnover	or	Balance sheet total
Medium-sized	< 250	≤ ☐ 50 m		≤ ☐ 43 m
Small	< 50	≤ ☐ 10 m		≤ ☐ 10 m
Micro	< 10	≤ ☐ 2 m		≤ ☐ 2 m

Food distribution

Sun Mark, UK, could be described as a "rags to riches" story that shows the benefits of hard work. Rami Ranger, owner and founder, started the business from a rented shed with start-up capital of just £2 (□2.40) and a £40 (□48) typewriter. The company has had to overcome HMS customs rigorous or stringent clearance rules and regulations to carve out a niche for itself in the overseas or foreign markets. Seventeen years later, the key to its global success is the excellent quality of its services and products coupled with competitive prices.

Sun Mark operates a global distribution network for some of the United Kingdom's most established and well-known **food brands**. It also manufactures its own line of high quality, value-for-money products.

Knowledge of local customs and tastes in individual markets has played a vital role in the company's growth in other countries. An important part of Sun Mark's success is that it is the only British company to have gained three consecutive Queen's Awards for "Enterprise in International Trade."

Asked what advice he has for entrepreneurs, Ranger said: "It is always wise not to put all your eggs in one basket; similarly, it is wise to do business in as many countries as possible in order to insulate oneself from the economic turmoil and political unrest of a particular country." Sun Mark has strongly diversified its international business, and today distributes its foods across Europe and to Africa, Asia, the Americas, and the Middle East.

Fashion designer

Paul Smith, the UK fashion designer and owner of fashion labels and retail stores Paul Smith, opened his first store at age twenty-four. He used his savings of 600 pounds (approx. US $810) to open a small twelve-foot-by-twelve-foot store because the bank had refused to loan him money.

Several years later, and with lots of determination, he had managed to secure a licensing agreement that paid him a small annual royalty of $15,000. That small but steady income stream had helped him pay the operating costs, avoid borrowing money, and build his business and brand slowly and prudently. The business is debt free, and current income stream comes from his retail shops, wholesaling, freelance, and consulting.

Presently, Japan is his biggest market, with annual sales in Japan amounting to $245 million. He has showrooms in London, Paris, Milan, New York, and Tokyo. His factories are located in Italy and England. There are about twelve different Paul Smith collections, such as: Paul Smith Women, Paul Smith Jeans, Paul Smith Accessories, Paul Smith Shoes, Paul Smith Watches, and Paul Smith Pens. Paul Smith china, rugs, spectacles, and fragrances are made under license.

In 2002, Paul collaborated with Cappellini to create the Mondo collection of furniture known as Paul Smith furniture. In 2003, Paul designed an upholstery textile in partnership with Maharam, called Bespoke. In September 2010, Paul opened his first stand-alone women's wear store in Mayfair, London.

The success of Paul Smith, one of the most solid fashion houses, can be attributed to owner Paul Smith's understanding of his role as a designer, retailer, and consultant, and his operating the business prudently. He is a hands-on operator—he is involved in all aspects of the business operations, designing clothes, choosing fabrics, approving retail store locations, and overseeing all developments within the company.

The questions below were prepared for you to test your strengths, weaknesses, and limitations. The answers that you write on the blank pages will become your *action plan*. It will help you to operate your business successfully.

1. **Some people have told me they were at work when they got fired. Some people have said they were home on a weekend, or they were on vacation and received a phone call from their employer informing them that their jobs, services, or positions were terminated. What do you plan to do if you are faced with a similar situation—if your job was outsourced or sent overseas ("offshoring")?**

    _____

    _____

    _____

    _____

2. **Would you start a business? Why do you want to start a business?**

_____

_____

3. **How did you get the idea to start a business?**

_____

_____

4. **Who has inspired you to start a business? (role model, if any)**

_____

_____

5. **What do you think is, or would be, your biggest challenge and why?**

_____

_____

6. **What are your strengths?**

_____

_____

7. **What are your weaknesses?**

_____

_____

8. **How do you plan to strengthen your weaknesses?**

_____

_____

The EU support for SMEs

During the European SMEs week in Brussels, the EU Commission released results and fact sheets that showed the progress of SMEs in all EU member states. They have shown that despite the challenging economic environment in Europe, SMEs held their ground and demonstrated that they were the backbone and powerhouse of the European economy and were the largest employers in the European Union.

SMEs represented more than 98 percent, or twenty-three million firms, and employed more than 85 percent, or 87 million employees. As a group, the twenty-three million SMEs are key drivers for economic growth, innovation, employment, and social integration. The European Commission aims to promote successful entrepreneurship and improve the business environment for SMEs to allow them to realize their full potential in a renewed economy.

The European Commission realizes that most SMEs are financed by bank loans, and borrowing is sometimes difficult for SMEs, especially when they do not have collateral, a track record, and a credit history, and oftentimes have a lifetime stigma, as an evil person is attached to a failed business owner, and the children of the failed business owner would sometimes have to carry their parent's stigma. That may sound silly or crazy to entrepreneurs in the United States of America, where failure is a learning process and a plus for trying. Hence, access to financing is crucial for twenty-three million SMEs that create 85 percent of jobs in the private sector. Also, complaints are frequently aired about the red tape created by European law. Hence, the commission has decided to take the following actions:

1. **Launch European SME Week** to promote entrepreneurship and facilitate the sharing of experiences, and to foster entrepreneurial attitudes.

2. **Cut red tape** and make it possible for individuals in all EU member states to pay 100 euros and start a new company in three business days instead of waiting for up to three years—the time it used to take to get approval to start a business in some member states.

3. **Reduce the administrative burden on SMEs.**

4. **Enforce the new EU directives** on late payment to SMEs. This will apply in all member states. SMEs must be paid in thirty to sixty days; not one year. After the sixty-day deadline, an 8 percent penalty will be imposed on debtors, because small companies will fail or die if they have to wait for one year to get payment for goods and services rendered, and tens of thousands of jobs will be lost; **and oftentimes a stigma will be attached to failure.**

5. **Help SMEs attract investors by sharing in the risks of borrowing.**

The EU Commission recognizes that certain groups of people in the society, especially migrants and ethnic minorities, who represent a large productive pool of people in Europe, have difficulties trying to start microenterprises, and firms such as craft enterprises can face specific problems. Hence, it has taken measures to help those groups and enterprises operate in the European marketplace by guaranteeing loans and encouraging investment companies to loan money to SMEs that have growth potential.

Many of the business problems that migrant and ethnic entrepreneurs face are generally shared by small business owners. However, the following problems appear to affect migrants and ethnic entrepreneurs:

a. Limited access to capital/finance and support services
b. Language barriers
c. Limited business management and marketing skills
d. Overconcentration of business in low-entry-threshold activities where the scope for expansion or diversification into the mainstream markets may be limited.

The EU commissioner has reported that member states have done a lot of work to tackle the problems of deliberate discrimination faced by migrants and ethnic minorities, but the problems that ethnic entrepreneurs face are mostly due to circumstance rather than discrimination.

The European Commission closely monitors the market for business loans and provides information to help businesses. It has earmarked over one billion euros to help SMEs grow. The funds are managed by **the European Investment Fund (EIF)** in cooperation with several intermediaries such as **banks, credit guarantors, and venture capital funds.** The EU expects over four hundred thousand SMEs will benefit from the financial scheme.

Owners of SMEs who need loan-guaranteed money to operate or grow their businesses can borrow at a very low interest rate from the EU Fund and pay the interest only in the first year of operation. Owners of SMEs who are facing temporary financial difficulties are given a grace period, during which they can postpone monthly payment of interest and principal on their loans. It is a win-win partnership.

6. Create the "Erasmus for Young Entrepreneurs" program. This program promotes the business sense or business savvy and talent of new EU entrepreneurs. It enables an individual to acquire practical skills or knowledge from an experienced entrepreneur in another country before setting up his/her own business. It also enables a business owner to acquire expertise that will give him/her the capabilities to manage his/her business. The program enables entrepreneurs from various countries to meet for three months. During that period of time, the mentor would offer business management knowledge, such as:

a. Strategic planning
b. Business organization
c. Explain services—types of customers and trends in the marketplace
d. Marketing strategies
e. Business and market development

Poaching of workers. A government plan aimed at preventing large corporations from poaching skilled workers from small and medium-sized enterprises has sparked controversy. In a bid to stem the brain drain plaguing SMEs, the Ministry of Employment and Labor is set to unveil a guideline on compensation that big businesses will be required to pay SMEs for recruiting their core employees.

The scheme is intended to address the free rider problem of large companies hiring away workers for whom SMEs have invested in training. The ministry's idea is that big corporations should either compensate SMEs for training costs or assume the burden of training new SME employees. The plan comes amid growing complaints among SMEs about outflows of their best employees. Early this year, the Korea Association of Machinery Industry urged the government to step up oversight of big firms' recruitment practices.

According to the Korea Small Business Institute, the migration of competent manpower from SMEs to large corporations began to increase after the government in 2006 removed the entry barriers to a group of business areas that had been preserved for SMEs.

Large corporations have poached top-notch workers at SMEs who could easily fit into their businesses. They lured the targeted employees with attractive pay packages and better working environments. As a result, turnover of skilled workers at SMEs rose sharply. According to a KSBI report, the rate jumped from 2.1 percent in 2008 to 5.11 percent in 2010.

SMEs lose competitive advantages when they lose their best workers. They are often forced to suspend their R&D programs, which disrupts their efforts to develop new products. This has led to a reduction in new orders, and that has brought many businesses to a halt. Even when some of those businesses have managed to survive, they are less inclined to invest in workplace training, as they have become more concerned about poaching. This dilemma has increased the shortages of competent workers.

To address this problem, the commission on shared growth for large and small companies set up in July a panel to mediate disputes between companies on worker recruitment. Yet, the panel has been largely ineffective. The ministry's solution basically calls on large companies to foster manpower themselves instead of trying to free ride on the efforts of SMEs. When they do have to recruit SME employees, they are required to pay compensation to cover the time and effort invested in training them.

The ministry will soon unveil schedules that specify the amounts of compensation for workers with different levels of expertise and specialties.

How this scheme will play out remains to be seen. But as the KFSMB argues, the measure cannot be a fundamental solution to the manpower outflow problem facing many domestic SMEs.

Even if large corporations, as hoped, refrain from luring workers from SMEs, some highly skilled employees may still decide to quit their jobs to earn more money and work in a healthier environment. There is no way to restrict workers' freedom to choose employment. Workers, whether skilled or not, shun SMEs primarily because of the ever-widening salary gap between SMEs and conglomerates. Therefore, any attempt to address the brain drain of SMEs will have to include measures to narrow the salary gap. The government needs to provide tax benefits and other incentives to skilled workers and R&D personnel at SMEs.

At the same time, the government needs to weed out nonviable SMEs to create room for the growth of competitive companies. Financial support to zombie SMEs should be withdrawn and be funneled to start-ups and promising SMEs. The government has been shying away from restructuring the SME sector. But without removing hopeless companies, it is difficult to boost the competitiveness of healthy SMEs.

I appreciate feedback from my readers and clients. My e-mail address is **ClemBarry@ aol.com**, and my website is **www.ConsultantBarry.com**.

CHAPTER 20
NGOS AND NONPROFITS

Government regulations, weak economies, low credit ratings, and increasing and fierce competition for scarce resources following deep budget cuts have hit NGOs and nonprofit organizations hard. This was prevalent during the worldwide economic recessions from 2007 to 2013. Governments around the world have had to face economic reforms and austerity measures that were imposed upon them by lending and regulatory institutions and agencies such as the IMF, World Bank, European Central Bank, and regulatory agencies such as Standard & Poor's and Fitch's.

NGOs

NGOs are nongovernmental organizations. An NGO is defined as any nonprofit voluntary citizens' group that is organized on a local, national, or international level. Task-oriented and driven by people with a common interest, NGOs perform a variety of service and humanitarian functions, bring citizen concerns to governments, advocate and monitor policies, and encourage political participation through provision of information. **Some are organized around specific issues, such as child labor laws, violence against women, the environment, health, and poverty-social protection programs**.

They provide analysis and expertise, serve as early-warning mechanisms and help monitor and implement international agreements. Their relationship with offices and agencies of the United Nations system differs depending on their goals, their venue, and the mandate of a particular institution.

Borrowing liberally from the World Bank's vague Operational Directive 14.70, **NGOs are defined as private organizations "characterized primarily by humanitarian or cooperative, rather than commercial, objectives**. They pursue activities to relieve suffering, promote the interests of the poor, protect the environment, provide basic social services, or undertake community development" in developing countries. NGOs are the subset of the broader nonprofit sector that is engaged specifically in international development. This definition excludes many of the active nonprofit organizations in developed countries, such as hospitals and universities.

Some data collectors have combined "community-based organization" with nongovernmental organizations. However, these categories are kept separate because, unlike nongovernmental organizations, community-based organizations exist to benefit their members directly. NGOs operate as a group that is active in the efforts of international development and increasing the welfare of poor people in poor countries. NGOs work both independently and alongside bilateral aid agencies from developed countries, private-sector infrastructure operators, self-help associations, and local governments.

Nonprofits

There are about twenty-five different types of 501(c) nonprofit organizations. Some of these charitable organizations provide similar services, and they compete for contributions from the public sector, private sector, and individuals.

Nonprofit charitable organizations are exempt under Section 501(c)(3) of the Internal Revenue Code. Other tax-exempt organizations covered in this section include those exempt under Sections 501(c)(4) through 501(c)(9).

Here is a short list of charitable organizations in the United States of America that are recognized by the Internal Revenue Service (IRS):

501(c)(3): religious, educational, charitable, scientific, and literary organizations, testing for public safety organizations and organizations for the prevention of cruelty to children and animals, fostering nationals, and international amateur sports competition.

501(c)(4): civic leagues, social welfare organizations, and local associations of employees.

501(c)(5): labor, agriculture, and horticultural organizations.

501(c)(6): Business leagues, chambers of commerce, and real estate boards.

501(c)(7): Social and recreational clubs.

501(c)(8): Fraternal beneficiary societies and associations.

501(c)(9): Voluntary employee beneficiary associations.

In the United States of America, an individual who gives donation(s) to charitable organizations can deduct on his/her tax return charitable contributions of 100 percent, 50 percent, 30 percent, or 20 percent of his/her adjusted gross income if s/he itemizes deductions. It depends on whether the donation is cash or property, and the kind of property that is donated. You should check with the Inland Revenue Service, Department of Revenue Services, or Department of Taxation, in your country.

A corporation can deduct charitable contributions that are up to 10 percent of its taxable income. Any amount that exceeds the 10 percent ceiling can be carried forward and used in future tax years. The deduction allowed for property that a corporation has contributed is the property's fair market value (FMV). However, the deduction is reduced for gifts of certain kinds of property.

Many nonprofit organizations are dependent on governments for partial contributions (one-third of their budgets) or full contributions to their budgets. During the economic recessions, nonprofit organizations had to compete for scarce resources against for-profit corporations that have lost their government contracts and switched to nonprofit status. In addition, many nonprofit organizations (colleges, churches, etc.) have had to return contributions that they had already spent because their donors were prosecuted for defrauding investors in Ponzi schemes.

A smaller or tighter government budget means nonprofit organizations would receive less money from governments. Some of them have received 3 percent to 20 percent less government funding. Those that used to be fully funded by government contributions have tried to bridge or close their budget gaps by soliciting philanthropic support from private and public foundations and individual donors who, in return, have demanded transparency. **Hence nonprofit organizations had to:**

1. **Restructure or streamline their programs.**
2. **Reduce their workforce.**
3. **Refuse to hire new workers (a freeze on hiring).**
4. **Provide the same amount of work with fewer resources (doing more with less).**
5. **Partner/collaborate with large for-profit corporations. The not-for profit organizations would do a needs assessment analysis and evaluate what services government grants would not be able to pay for. To close their budget gaps, they would approach the large for-profit corporations for help in the form of:**

   a. **Funding.** (A not-for-profit organization provides services for a large for-profit corporation. In exchange, the latter pays for advertising and marketing for the former.)
   b. **Consultancy.** (A not-for-profit organization provides services for a large for-profit corporation. In exchange, the former receives accounting and advisory services.)
   c. **Volunteers.** (A not-for-profit organization provides services to a for-profit corporation. The for-profit corporation allows its workers to volunteer and build a stage for the former or help the former raise funds during its fund-raising drives.

In addition, not-for-profit organizations are hit with more and new regulations and higher levels of accountability. The reforming of Form 990 and the Sarbanes-Oxley Act have continued to be a hurdle for nonprofit organizations, and they have responded by ensuring that what they are doing is documented and reported in their annual reports. Many nonprofit organizations have adopted the habit of:

1. Posting completed Forms 990 on their websites
2. Posting full-blown audited financial statements on their websites

Board members have become more sophisticated about:

1. Who they choose to sit on the board
2. How they select their members

Board members and donors are aware of their responsibilities, and they have become more financially astute. Hence, when sophisticated people are involved with preparing and investigating financial reports, the members can count on receiving better advice and results.

Donors should check with their country's Better Business Bureau, Department of Consumer Affairs, or foreign mission/embassy before sending donations or other charitable relief to any organization. The Better Business Bureau's Wise Give Alliance urges donors to scrutinize charitable organizations before making any donation.

Donors should be concerned about avoiding fraud, and they also need to ensure that their money goes to competent charitable and relief organizations that are equipped and experienced to handle the unique challenges of providing assistance. Donors who would like to research charitable organizations to see if they exist or are legitimate can log on to the website of Better Business: **www.bbb.org/charity**

I appreciate feedback from my readers and clients. My e-mail address is **ClemBarry@ aol.com**, and my website is **www.ConsultantBarry.com**.

CHAPTER 21
BUYING A BUSINESS

"If you are searching for well-cut diamonds, you may never find diamonds in the rough."

Read the whole chapter just like you would read a newspaper or novel; then come back and answer the questions. The answers that you write on the blank pages will become your *action plan*. It will help you to operate your business successfully.

A person who has the financial resources would prefer to buy a business instead of starting one because of the risks and hard work that are involved with starting a business and waiting for many years to make a profit. Apart from have a strong background about how businesses operate, it is important to understand the operations of the business you want to buy and the industry in which it operates. Businesses in various industries operate differently.

When I was starting out in taxation, a seasoned tax professional told me: "There is a big difference between knowing how to operate a business and knowing how to operate this business."

The following character traits are important if you want to become successful in any business, whether the business is a start-up, an existing business that you have bought, or a franchise.

1. You must do your research about the business and the industry.
2. You must be intelligent, focus, and have financial discipline.
3. You must be versatile and have a strong work ethic.

4. You must be a problem-solver. Owning a business comes with challenges and responsibilities.

5. You must be able to provide **exceptional service** to keep customers coming back. Hence, you must like the industry that you are about to enter. You must have a good personality, like what you do, **be a resource for customers** (be very knowledgeable), and be engaging with customers, suppliers, creditors, employees, shareholders, partners, and government workers.

You have decided to buy a business, and you are determined to find out how your competitors are doing. You have decided to visit their stores as a mystery shopper and experience for yourself why customers do business with them and what their strengths and weaknesses are in the industry. Use the following survey format to prepare your report:

Point of Purchase Analysis

1. Store layout and ease of location selection

_____

_____

2. Store cleanliness

_____

_____

3. Depth of product selection (product lines)

_____

_____

_____

4. Employees' appearance

_____

_____

_____

5. **Employees' approach (work ethic)**

_____

_____

_____

6. **Employees' knowledge of products (training)**

_____

_____

7. **Advice on or about customer care**

_____

_____

8. **Product(s) recommendations (outside brands and store brand)**

_____

_____

_____

9. **After-sale service programs (warranty, return policy, etc.)**

_____

_____

10. **Cash and wrap area appearance**

_____

_____

_____

11. **General/overall service level**

_____

_____

_____

12. **Telephone surveys**

_____

_____

_____

13. Market research projects undertaken

_____

_____

_____

14. Exit polls

_____

_____

15. Customer service audits

_____

_____

_____

If you have the money or can obtain a loan from a bank to make the down payment and have a reserve to pay your operation costs for three to six months, then buying an existing business that has a steady customer base and generates a strong daily or weekly cash flow to pay its overhead expenses will help you recoup your investment quickly. If such a business is for sale, then your first priority is to do your due diligence before you fall in love with the business. That means you are required to do your homework before you make the purchase.

1. **The first step** is to do a survey of your competitors (see survey format above).
2. Make an appointment with the sellers/owners and interview them about why they are selling the business, the business location, the date the lease will expire, the amount of money that they owe financial institutions and suppliers, any business tax return that they did not file, existing insurance coverage, business taxes that are pending, name of their business bank, pending lawsuits, etc. During this process, the seller would prescreen you to ensure that you are qualified to buy the business.
3. Ensure that the business is a good or right fit for you.
4. Introduce members of your family to the owners and the business and have them talk with the owner(s) while they survey the business and provide you with some feedback.
5. Get authorization from the seller to contact the business customers, creditors, and suppliers.

6. Get an appraisal of the business—business valuation. **Business valuation** is the appraisal of the economic value of a business.

Who would need a business valuation report?

Buyers, partners, courts, taxing authorities, creditors, and investors would need it.

When is a business valuation report required?

1. Buying, merging, or selling a business
2. Divorce proceedings
3. Estate planning and probate
4. Partner(s) entering and exiting
5. Filing for bankruptcy and reorganization
6. Tax purposes (evaluating capital gains or losses)
7. Verification of worth (bankers and investors)
8. Private placement and initial public offering

When will the report be available?

From three days to ninety days. It depends on how quickly you provide us with the necessary information, how quickly we can have access to the business, and how quickly you pay us.

1. Have your accountant help you negotiate the final purchase price of the business before you make a down payment. Your accountant will collect and review five years of business tax returns and financial statements, and check for business and employment taxes owed to the taxing authorities. If you are happy with what the accountant tells you, then negotiations for purchasing the business can begin. During negotiation the sellers would want you to provide proof that you can raise the money to buy the business. If you have access to the money to buy the business, the sellers would request that you put the money in escrow with your attorney or their attorney. The rule of thumb when buying an existing

business is making a down payment of no more than 33 percent of the selling price of the business.

2. **This step is very important**. Before you make a down payment on the business, ask you attorney whether the **consumer fraud act** in your state or country applies to the sale of an ongoing or existing business. If it does or does not, and you want to buy the business, have your attorney draw up an installment agreement for **seller's financing** that requires the owner(s) of the business to accept 33 percent down payment and remain/stay in the business with you for one to six months. **Depending on the size of the business, the duration of time that the owner(s) will have to spend teaching you the business is negotiable.** During that time you are gradually paying off the owner(s) for the business as stipulated in the installment agreement while you are getting acquainted with the customers and learning about the business and systems of operation.

3. Keep the existing business name or take down the sign and replace it with a new sign and a new business name. In either case, you will be required to prepare and file documents with your state or country's department of corporation or business, **notifying the government authorities of the change of ownership and the status of the new business (S-corporation, C-corporation, partnership, LLC, etc.)**.

4. Open a new business bank account.

5. Reorganize the business, and contact or meet with the existing customers and suppliers.

6. Shop around for new suppliers and decide whether you want to do business with new suppliers or keep the old suppliers.

7. Focus on techniques that will help you generate revenue while you are skillfully managing the operating expenses.

8. Have a monthly agreement with your accountant or tax advisor or board of advisors. (See chapter on business advisors.)

Hardware store

A prospective buyer wanted to buy a business. He found a seller who felt it was necessary to downsize and keep fewer stores. The seller sold him a hardware store. The store has sixty employees and has been in operation for over twenty years. The buyer used creative financing to acquire the business from the seller. Here is how it works:

1. **The seller agreed to keep 30 percent** of the business for two years **(seller financing)** after he did his due diligence and was happy about the prospective buyer's credibility and his ability to operate and manage a business. The seller also encouraged his suppliers to ship merchandise on credit to the buyer or new owner.

2. **The buyer kept 30 percent** of the company and sold his remaining 40 percent of the company to his suppliers and workers in the company as follows:

   Operations manager—5 percent
   Accountant—15 percent
   Warehouse manager—5 percent
   Sales manager—5 percent
   Suppliers—10 percent

All sixty workers remained with the company. With help from the seller, the new owners developed a business model and an aggressive three-year marketing plan to recover 70 percent of the market share that was lost to competitors. They planned to increase market share in new and underserved niches by 20 percent. The suppliers were intrigued, and they purchased the remaining 10 percent stake in the business and allowed him to use their connections to grow the company faster.

Transactions like that are common in many industries. There are people who have owned their first business that way. The owners of the company that you are working for may own other companies that they plan to sell two years from now. They know your capabilities and work ethic, and they will be happy to work with you if you approach them with this strategy to buy their company.

I appreciate feedback from my readers and clients. My e-mail address is **ClemBarry@ aol.com**, and my website is **www.ConsultantBarry.com**.

CHAPTER 22
BUYING A FRANCHISE

In the United States of America, franchise owners collectively employ eight million people. Buying a franchise does provide the franchisee or entrepreneur with an opportunity to own and operate a business that has a proven and successful formula. That formula was built from many years of research and testing, and it cannot be easily duplicated by the entrepreneur.

A person or investor who has the financial resources would prefer to own a franchise instead of starting a business because the risks associated with starting a business are high, and the investor would have to wait many years to make a profit and achieve his or her goals. However, it is important to note that there are many failed franchisees. They are listed in the "Franchise Offering Circular" that every franchisor must give you when you state your intention to buy a franchise from them.

Owning a franchise means you have established a business relationship with a successful company that would help you get a quick return on your investment. **You have purchased a license** from the franchisor, and you agree to pay **an initial fee plus an annual franchise fee of 3 percent to 10 percent of business income** to the franchisor for using its name, training, support, operating systems, and marketing systems to sell its products or services during the term of the franchise agreement.

Here are some of the reasons people buy franchises:

1. The name and brand is well known and easily recognized.
2. There is a predetermine menu and a customer base.

3. The program and concepts have been tested and constantly improved, and the method is successful.

4. The franchisor has been operating successful franchisees for many years, so you just have to follow the procedures.

5. Being part of a franchise reduces the learning curve and the time it would take to become successful.

6. A franchise can keep you from getting into trouble with the law if you are new to a country, and you are not knowledgeable about business operations and employment laws in that country.

Be sure to do your research or homework before you buy a franchise. Google the names of the franchisors in your market from which you would like to buy a franchise. If you would like to buy a **product franchise,** such as a hamburger franchise, then get the names of several hamburger franchisors that you would like to buy a franchise from, and do your research on everybody. Use this procedure to evaluate **service franchisors** too.

Here is what one employee who had worked for nineteen years for an established franchisor had to say:

"Every time there is a drop in sales, problems with merchandising, or difficulty rolling out new products, the franchisor would blame the franchisees and unit managers. Instead of the company developing and implementing original ideas or starting to listen to its franchisees for specific marketing ideas, it just keep copying its competitors and remaining one step behind. Apparently those at the top feel it is easier for the company to rely on its brand name than work harder and compete for first place. I'm sure things over there haven't changed that much since I left."

Fill out the questionnaire below. The answers that you write will become your *action plan*. It will help you decide if a particular franchise is suitable for you.

Point of Purchase and Taste Analysis

1. Have you ever shopped or dined at the franchise? Yes____ No ___
2. How often do you shop or dine at the franchise? _____
3. o you like the products or food? Yes___ No _____

4. Do you like the service? Yes _____ No ____

5. How would you describe customer traffic? High__ Moderate____ Slow__

6. Do you believe the price would attract new customers? Yes____ No__

7. What feedback did you get from customers whom you met there?

    _____

    _____

8. Would you like to purchase a franchise? Yes_____ No ____

9. Does the franchise match your personality? Yes _____ No ___

10. Do you have the funds to purchase a franchise? Yes __ No __

Call the franchisor and express your interest in becoming a franchisee. Ask for a copy of the financial statement and a copy of their franchise offering circular.

11. Review the information with an accountant and an attorney.

    _____

    _____

    _____

    _____

12. Pay close attention to the number of franchisees who have had disputes and filed lawsuits against the franchisor. Call the franchisees and talk to them and take notes. You will be surprised how much information a disappointed franchisee would give you.

    _____

    _____

    _____

    _____

13. Pay attention to the number of franchisees who have gone out of business and are angry with the franchisor. Call those franchisees and take notes of the information they are giving you. They are angry, and they will not hold back anything, so it is to your advantage to extract important information from them.

    _____

    _____

    _____

    _____

14. Look at the franchisor's training and supplies policy.

_____

_____

_____

_____

15. Look at the price of the franchise, the franchise fee, and the franchise royalty fee that you are required to pay. Those are usually the cause of disputes between franchisors and franchisees. Call those angry franchisees and get feedback from them and take notes.

_____

_____

_____

_____

16. If you are interested in buying a franchise, make an appointment with the franchisor to discuss buying a franchise and to clarify the information that you have obtained from your research and reliable sources. Make notes here:

_____

_____

_____

_____

Here are some additional questions that you should ask every franchisor. Please be patient and take notes.

When I buy a franchise from you:

1. Would I become my own boss?

_____

_____

2. Would other franchise owners be my competitors or associates?

_____

_____

3. How large would be my exclusive territory?

_____

_____

4. Do I need special skills and training to operate the franchise?

_____

_____

I appreciate feedback from my readers and clients. My e-mail address is **ClemBarry@ aol.com**, and my website is **www.ConsultantBarry.com**.

CHAPTER 23

BANKING

Read the whole chapter just like you would read a newspaper or novel; then come back and answer the questions. The answers that you write on the blank pages will become your *action plan*. It will help you to operate your business successfully.

1. The importance of a banking relationship
2. Choosing the best bank for your business
3. When and how to approach a bank for funding
4. The importance of a business valuation report
5. The importance of letters of credit

Banks

Apart from having a good relationship with your employees, customers, suppliers, accountant, tax advisor, and attorney, it is imperative that you have a strong relationship with your business or commercial account manager at your bank.

Question

How do you build a profitable business relationship with a banker?

Answer

Banks, like all businesses, are in business to make a profit. Every item in the bank's product line, including minimum deposits, money markets, retirement plans, factoring of accounts receivable, mortgages, personal and business loans, payroll service, life insurance, etc., is put there so that the banker would sell them to customers and make a profit for the bank and make a commission for himself/herself. **Therefore, you must find out from the banker what you would have to do to maintain a profitable banking relationship with the bank, and then negotiate and give the banker the items that would make the bank profitable and reduce your cost of doing business with the bank**. **This is a strategy that benefits the bank and your business**. For example, how would you be able to get free checking? You may be required to keep a minimum monthly balance in your business checking account and not perform more than one hundred, two hundred or five hundred transactions per month. How would you be able to get a business loan without providing any documentation? You may be required to have a minimum balance in your business checking account. You may be required to transfer some or all of your investments to the bank. You may be required to allow the bank to manage you accounts receivable or sell your accounts receivable to the bank (accounts receivable factoring).

Banks will take deposits from virtually any business that operates in any industry. However, they have different lending criteria for businesses in different industries. Don't be fooled into believing that because your bank teller smiles at you and is friendly with you when you go into the bank to make your deposits that you would be able to get a loan from that bank when your business needs it. Banks will tell you that they lend money to small businesses, but don't be fooled into believing that your small business will get a loan when you apply for it.

When you apply for a business loan or revolving line of credit, you will be surprised to learn that the bank that has been taking your deposits has turned you down or denied your application because, oftentimes, bankers don't understand your business and the industry in which it operates.

Farmers, estate owners, and people in agriculture prefer to do business with a "farmers' bank" because bankers there grew up on farms, and they understand the industry and the seasonality of the business. As a small-business owner, it is advisable that you do business with a bank that meets these three criteria:

1. A bank that understands your industry and business operations
2. A bank that has recently financed businesses in your industry
3. A bank that has a history of financing businesses in your industry

There are banks that would approve a business loan or revolving line of credit for SMEs, small companies, and university spin-offs, in a certain industry, at their early or growth stage; and there are banks that would not approve a loan for the same businesses in their early-growth stage. Banks have claimed that certain industry is too risky or cyclical. In that case, the loan manager would suggest that the business owner:

1. Borrows money from his/her savings account
2. Takes a loan against his/her pension
3. Takes a loan against the assets of the business
4. Applies for a home equity line of credit, whereby the owner's home or a rental property that belongs to the owner is used as collateral or security for the loan.

Interest rate basics

1. General

When you borrow money from a lender for a period of time, you will be required to pay a price for using the lender's money. This price, or borrowing cost, is called interest. A high or low interest rate is determined by the economic forces of demand and supply. Low interest rates encourage more borrowers to seek out lenders and start businesses. A low interest rate is a prelude to creating new jobs and hiring more workers and contractors as new orders for goods and services increase, and companies borrow more money to build offices and plants and buy new tools and equipment to increase production. Interest rates will rise steadily as economic activities increase, and the economy becomes stronger and more vibrant. Hence, the rate of interest that you will pay for using a lender's money will depend on how slow or vibrant the economy is and on your ability to repay the lender in monthly installments.

2. The Federal Reserve Bank

In the United States of America, the Federal Reserve Bank lowers short-term interest rates to reduce long-term borrowing costs to savings and commercial banks. Lower rates are beneficial to banks that have portfolios of underperforming loans, and they also encourage the federal government to borrow money for infrastructure development. The lower rate is also passed on to borrowers to encourage them to stimulate economic growth. This usually encourages inflation, whereby people must spend a bigger portion of their earnings to buy the same amount of goods and services. For example, a gallon of diesel fuel that increases by four cents can cost a truck owner $5,000 more a year for fuel to operate the same truck plying the same route. Hence, as the economy gets hot, higher interest rates are steadily introduced to cool it.

3. Central banks

When the Federal Reserve Bank and central banks around the world are printing too much money, the price of goods and services will increase drastically, and investors will become nervous and concerned that the currencies that they are holding will lose value to inflation. Hence, they will demand a high interest rate from borrowers. Some investors will lose faith and exchange currencies they are holding for other reliable currencies, and sometimes they will sell their investments early in some countries and cut their losses.

Letter of credit and bank draft

A letter of credit is a safe way for collecting payment from overseas consignees. A letter of credit should be used by the seller if the seller plans to ship merchandise to a consignee for more than a year. It is used to establish long business transactions. Letters of credit are usually not used for shipment by air because the merchandise will arrive quickly and incur storage/demurrage charges at the airport while the letter of credit documents take several weeks to arrive before the shipment can be cleared.

Use letters of credit for all overseas customers with whom you do not have a history. Ensure everything in the letter of credit is set up the way you want it at the beginning of the process and request that a draft of the letter of credit be sent to you.

When you, the consignor, fill out the terms of the letter of credit, it becomes the responsibility of the customer's or consignee's bank (opening bank) to pay you, because it had secured the letter of credit. Hence, before the merchandise is shipped you should discuss with your customer what you will ship and the terms and conditions, and incorporated them in the letter of credit.

1. A good practice before issuing a letter of credit is to send the bank draft to the receiving party and to allow a few days for the draft to be confirmed by that party and their bank, and then officially issue the letter of credit via SWIFT.
2. A smart thing to do is to have the letter of credit paid to your bank instead of to the customer's or consignee's bank (opener's bank). By doing this, you can communicate with your bankers more easily than depending on the opener's bank to raise discrepancies.
3. Another way to ensure that you receive payment is to make the customer's bank the consignee on the letter of credit. Hence, if there is a discrepancy, you will get paid.
4. Another secure way is to take out trade credit Insurance.

Depending on the country from which you are shipping the merchandise, a smart term that you can use in your letters of credit is, "country should be confirmed by a USA bank, or a Swiss bank or a UBS bank." You are asking one of the international banks to guarantee payment upon presentation of conforming documents. However, if there is a discrepancy in the terms and conditions outlined in the letter of credit the consignee / customer would be allowed to accept the documents before honoring the letter of credit and paying for the merchandise/shipment. Be careful with the terms of sale that you use on the letter of credit. If you say payment at sight plus forty-five days, that means you are prepared to accept payment forty-five days after the presentation date on the draft. Contact your bank for details.

Getting a business loan

Question

When a business owner applies for a loan, what does the bank look for?

Answer

The bank is concerned about the business owner's ability to repay the loan.

This is usually based on the three Cs (character, collateral, and credit).

Sometimes a bank would require that the business owner sign a personal guarantee to secure a business loan. If a bank wants you to do that, then it means the bank wants to look beyond your business financial statements and business plan and into your personal finances, tax returns, and credit reports. The rationale is if the business owner does not pay his/her mortgage, loans, and bills at home, then the probability is high that he/she will not pay the bills for the business.

I have asked loan managers at major banks Wells Fargo, Citi Bank, Barclays Bank, Bank of Canada, Bank of Ireland, JPMorgan Chase and Bank of America about the lending criteria that they use to loan money to their small business customers. Here is a summary of the four requirements that a business customer must meet before a loan application is approved.

1. Every customer must completely fill out a loan or credit application form.

   a. What is the purpose of the loan?

   _____
   _____
   _____
   _____

   b. How would the loan or revolving line of credit be used in the business?

   _____
   _____
   _____
   _____

   c. How would the loan help the business?

   _____
   _____
   _____
   _____

      1) Are you looking to expand or develop your business activities?

      2) Do you want to introduce innovations?

3) Do you want to finance R&D?

4) Do you want to acquire new technology?

5) Would the loan be used to finance working capital?

6) Would the loan be used to buy inventory?

7) Would the loan be used to pay for equipment?

8) Would it be a short-term or long-term loan?

2. Is the size of the loan that I am requesting a realistic amount?

3. Does the loan fit the business needs? For example, asking a bank for a loan of $200,000 when your business can only service or repay a loan of $150,000. In this case the bank can modify your loan requirement and offer you the amount of the loan your business is qualified for, or it can consider your loan application fraudulent and shred your application.

4. The credit history of the applicant and the business is of utmost importance. An applicant for a bank loan should review credit reports and correct errors on the reports. If you had overextended your personal and/or business loans, credit limit, or credit card limit, you should pay down the debts before you apply for a loan from a bank or financial institution.

Banks and financial institutions want to extend credit or loans to customers who:

a. Honor their loan obligation in a timely manner—customers who pay the bank on time.
b. Control or manage the amount of outstanding debts effectively.
c. Maintain a good vendor relationship with the bank, suppliers, and other creditors.

5. Company finances: The bank would review your company's income statement, tax returns, credit history, and financial history. It is important that your personal and business financial data is accurate, and those data reflect your and your business's current financial situation. The bank will use those data to calculate the business's solvency ratios and determine if your business is qualified as a going concern—if it meets the requirements of the going concern concept. The bank would like to know the kind and value of the collateral that you want to use to secure the loan. Finally, the loan manager may request more documentation and information from you, request a face-to-face meeting with you, and take a tour of your business to get a feel of the true nature of the business. Either way, you will be informed about the status of the loan.

Loan managers whom I have met with have told me that when a longstanding customer whom the bank has had a good banking relationship with applies for a loan or revolving line of credit, they would take a cautious approach. They would encourage the customer to continue making the daily deposit, and they would closely monitor the flow of those daily deposits and cover the customer's withdrawals as the bank deemed necessary, economical, and safe until the customer makes the next daily deposit to cover the shortage or overdraft for the previous day. The bank does not want to be left holding on to an empty bag.

When you have found a bank that would meet your business needs, go ahead and open your new business bank account. Take to the bank the certificate of partnership or incorporation and the business federal identification number that you have received from the government (state and IRS) when you registered your business. Fill out a bank application form and hand over all your documents and initial deposit to the bank employee. The application is processed, and you will be given a business account number and an address where you can order blank business checks. Some banks will have your business sign up for electronic deposit and withdrawal, whereby your business can accept checks, and credit and debit cards payments, from its customers and pay its creditors and suppliers automatically. This process will free up your time, and you will have more time to spend operating your business and acquiring more customers.

6. **Business valuation** is the appraisal of the economic value of a business.

Who would need a business valuation report?

Buyer, partners, courts, taxing authorities, creditors, and investors would need it.

When is a business valuation report required?

1. Buying, merging, or selling a business
2. Divorce proceedings
3. Estate planning and probate
4. Partner(s) entering and exiting
5. Filing for bankruptcy and reorganization
6. Tax purposes (evaluating capital gains or losses)
7. Verification of worth (bankers and investors)
8. Private placement and initial public offering

When will the report be available?

From three days to ninety days. It depends on how quickly you provide us with the necessary information, how quickly we can have access to the business, and how quickly you pay us.

I appreciate feedback from my readers and clients. My e-mail address is **ClemBarry@ aol.com**, and my website is **www.ConsultantBarry.com**.

CHAPTER 24
RAISING CAPITAL

You can finance your business as follows:

1. Use your own money (self-finance)
2. Use other people's credit (get a cosigner)
3. Crowd funding
4. Accept a partner
5. Angel investor
6. Venture capital
7. Employee stock ownership plan (ESOP)
8. Joint venture
9. Private placement.
10. Mezzanine financing
11. Junior stock market
12. Initial public offering

Self-finance

How did some start-ups finance their venture?

1. They borrowed from their savings, severance pay, pension, inheritance, home equity, credit cards, and the cash value from their whole life insurance policies.
2. They sold or pawned some of their assets/prized possessions.

Use a cosigner

If a borrower needs the service of a cosigner, then the borrower is high risk, and the lender could not ascertain that the borrower will repay the loan. If somebody cosigns on a loan for you, then that loan would appear as an outstanding debt on his or her credit report, and it will reduce his or her eligibility to qualify for other loans. If you default on the loan, the lender can sue the cosigner, and the court's judgment against the cosigner would become a lien against his/her possessions, and his/her belongings will be sold to satisfy your debt. The cosigner may also be required to pay legal fees that the lender incurred to pursue the case. That can hurt the cosigner's FICO scores and future employment position, as employers would evaluate his/her credibility and question his/her judgment. Those are some of the reasons why a lot of people would not cosign for anybody.

Goldman Sachs 10,000 Small Businesses program

In the United States of America, Goldman Sachs *10,000 Small Businesses program* is a $500 million investment to help entrepreneurs create jobs and economic opportunity. It provides quick access to education, financial capital, and business support services for small business owners. If your business has a minimum of four employees and generates income of $150,000 to $4 million a year, you may be eligible for the program. The program is currently operating in Chicago, Cleveland, Houston, Long Beach, Los Angeles, New Orleans, New York, Philadelphia, and Salt Lake City. Contact the Small Business Administration, **http://www.sba.gov.**

Crowd funding

Crowd funding is hailed as "the financing for the future." There is a dire need for investments in start-ups and high-growth companies, and crowd funding enables business start-ups and existing small businesses to tap into sources of capital other than bank loans, venture capitalists, and angel funds to raise capital or funding from multiple sources, including small amounts of money, say $300, from small investors.

Small companies can "test the waters" by making pitches to people in their network and beyond to discover the kinds of opportunities and funding that exist. They can use crowd funding for presales, to test the demand for a new product. Usually when they are seeking bank loans and venture capital to start their business or produce a product, they would have to prove that they have a profitable and solid idea. However, with crowd funding, small companies have the opportunity to prove that there is a need and a demand for a product, and investors who believe in the idea would invest in the idea or finance the venture.

For example, to design and produce the Nano-Light, a revolutionary lightbulb that produces the same amount of light as a conventional incandescent 100 watt lamp but consumes only 12 watts, a team of engineers in San Diego raised funding through crowd-funding website Kickstarter.com. The project reached its target of $20,000, and it also convinced 2,170 users to donate over $100,000 two weeks before bidding ended.

For-profit and non-for-profit businesses that are seeking crowd funding must:

1. Keep their presentation simple
2. Take the people who invest in their idea seriously

Profit and nonprofit businesses can receive money from ordinary investors through crowd funding websites such as Kickstarter.com, IndieGoGo.com and RocketHub.com. There are over two hundred crowd funding sites in Europe.

Accept a partner

1. A successful business owner once told me: "The hardest ship to keep afloat is a partnership."
2. "A relationship without trust is like a car without gas; you can stay in it for as long as you want, but it will never go anywhere."

Handling relationships

Priority #1, Preparation

If you are planning to share your business with a partner or investor, the accountant who is representing that person or business would pay more attention to unaudited financial statements. If you did not perform an audit of your business previously, then you should be prepared for increased scrutiny of your business book, records, and operations during the due diligence prior to agreement.

You goal should be to search for and select a partner or investor who can see the big picture and who you can trust. Every potential partner should be able to complement your skills and have the same business goals, ethics, financial mind-set, and professional and entrepreneurial drive or synergy as you. Have all potential partners or investors sign a confidentiality agreement and a noncompete agreement (covenant not to compete agreement) before you disclose anything about the business to them.

Priority # 2, Get Everything in Writing

There was a time when verbal agreements were respected, and a person's word was his/her bond. Nowadays most people would verbally agree to something and later deny they had ever agreed to anything. They don't care how much their actions hurt other people's businesses and feelings as long as their actions boost their egos. **This world is full of sociopaths**.

Get your potential partners to fill out a questionnaire like the one shown below. Get the names of people whom your potential partner or investor has worked for/with. Verify the information and have a private investigator do background checks on everybody. You do not want to partner with anybody who has a questionable background. That is not good for the business, and your life could be at stake. If you are satisfied with the results, then have your potential partner(s) sign a partnership agreement. The agreement should have a **buyout clause** in case you and your partner want to terminate the relationship. Make the agreement simple and clear so that both of you are comfortable working together. Also, every three to six months do a background check on all your partners.

#1 Partner or Investor

Name_____ Address_____

Cell phone _____ Fax_____

Business address_____

E-mail address_____

Website address_____

Specify your potential partner's or investor's primary skill _____

_____

Specify your potential partner's or investor's special knowledge _____

_____

Specify the amount of capital s/he must contribute $_____

Describe how you plan to use the capital that your partner will contribute to the

business_____

_____

_____

_____

#2 Partner or Investor

Name_____ Address_____

Cell phone _____ Fax_____

Business address_____

E-mail address_____

Website address_____

Specify your potential partner's or investor's primary skill _____

_____

Specify your potential partner's or investor's special knowledge _____

_____

Specify the amount of capital s/he must contribute $_____

Describe how you plan to use the capital that your partner will contribute to the

business_____

_____

_____

_____

Angel Investors

Angel investors like to invest in strong business owners whom they like and trust. They like business owners that have great products, clear visions, realistic business plans, and solid business models. They invest their money in businesses with the expectation of receiving their capital back plus a big return on their investments. They would usually invest their money into businesses and allow the owners to operate those businesses without interfering in the daily business operations, unless their opinion and expertise are requested. It is imperative that the business owner assemble a team of people to help negotiate with angel investors.

Venture capital

Venture capital investors like to invest in businesses that have great products, solid business models, and clear business strategies. They prefer to invest in industries that they are quite familiar with, and they want to become part of the management team and help operate the business. They bring to the business sound strategic thinking, valuable connections, market expertise, practical knowledge about what the business owner wants to accomplish, and money and a strategy to maximize the company's value. They will usually sell their shares through initial public offerings (IPOs) and exit the company. Hence, it is important that the business owner and the venture capitalist clearly understand the motive and intention of each other, and the objectives, financial goals, and strategic plan of the business. It is imperative that the business owner assembly a team of people to help negotiate with the venture capitalist.

Employee Stock Ownership Plan (ESOP)

If your business is profitable, you can establish this plan as an incentive to boost your employees' moral and increase their productivity by allowing them to buy your company's stocks and become investors in your company. This plan enables business owners to raise capital from inside the company to acquire other companies and to pay off existing shareholders.

Mezzanine financing

It is a combination of debt and equity financing that is typically used by real estate developers and leverage buyouts because it is sometimes easier for them to get financing from other sources. It is also used to finance the expansion of existing companies whereby the company issues debt that investors can convert into equity if the debt is not repaid. This kind of debt financing is low risk because it can be converted into equity in the company. However, it carries a higher interest rate than most secured debts because it is not secured with collateral.

Private placement

This is a privately negotiated financial transaction. It is designed to meet the specific need of a company that is not ready to go public but needs to obtain financing now from a large institutional investor such as pension funds, investment bankers, insurance companies, and money management funds, or from a small number of private investors that includes business acquaintance, neighbors, and friends. News about a company seeking private placement financing is equivalent to a tip-off that the company is preparing for an initial public offering. Investors who are searching for an opportunity to invest their money will jump at the chance to get in early with the expectation that they will benefit as new investors and speculators continue to bid the price higher. It is imperative that the business owner assembly a team of people to help him/her negotiate this transaction.

Initial public offering (IPO)

Advantages:

The dream of many small-business owners is to take their companies public and reap the advantages of raising capital on the stock market to expand the business. The sale of the company shares to the public by the company generates money that does not have to be paid back. The owners or founders of the company can sell some of their shares and recoup their initial investments. Venture capitalists and other investors can sell their shares and exit the company, and employees who had received stock options, stock appreciation rights, and stock bonuses as incentives can reward themselves financially by selling some of their shares as new investors and speculators continue to bid the price higher than the initial offering price.

Disadvantages:

Kenneth Cole seeks to buy back his own company

NEW YORK, 2013—Fashion designer Kenneth Cole is offering to pay about $148.5 million to buy back his publicly traded company, Kenneth Cole Productions Inc., saying his company would compete more effectively as a privately held company. He believes his company's shareholders and the stock market are too focused on short-term results—too much pressure to keep the stock price consistently rising every quarter. Cole, who serves as chairman and chief creative officer, currently holds about 47 percent of the stock and approximately 89 percent of its voting power. He was smart to keep a large percentage (majority share) of the company and 89 percent of the voting rights.

Michael Dell wants to take his company private.

In February 2013, Michael Dell, the founder of the world's third-largest PC-maker, announced he planned to buy back his publicly traded company from shareholders. He believes if his company becomes a private company he would have a freer hand to restructure the company without getting pressure from worried shareholders to constantly increase quarterly earnings. He wants to cut ties with the stockholders so he can do what is best for the company's longevity and future growth, and it is very difficult to do this in a publicly traded company. In 2011 Dell owned 243.35 million shares of his company's stock, which were worth $3.5 billion, giving him 12 percent ownership of the company. He sold 88 percent of the company and kept 12 percent. His shareholders could have banded together and voted him out of the company. Instead, in September 2013, they agreed with his offer per share, and they bought into his long-term vision of the company.

George Zimmer, founder of Men's Warehouse, was fired from the company he has taken forty years to build.

New York, 2013—Men's Warehouse gave no reason for the abrupt firing of George Zimmer, who has built Men's Warehouse from one small store to one of North America's largest specialty men's clothing stores, with 1,143 locations. On the day he was fired, George Zimmer owned 1.8 million shares, or 4 percent of the company. His mistakes were selling too much of the company, and he didn't have much voting power. He should have sold 40 percent of the company and keep 60 percent (majority share), plus 60 percent or more of the voting power.

I appreciate feedback from my readers and clients. My e-mail address is **ClemBarry@ aol.com**, and my website is **www.ConsultantBarry.com**.

CHAPTER 25
TECHNOLOGY

You will read about:

1. Cloud computing, crowd funding—the financing of the future—the importance of a modernized website, businesses planning, and office in home
2. Businesses that failed to reinvent themselves and had to struggle to survive and thrive in a changing business environment
3. A business that envisioned changes in the consumers' market and focus on innovation

Read the whole chapter just like you would read a newspaper or novel; then come back and answer the questions. The answers that you write on the blank pages will become your *action plan*. It will help you to operate your business successfully.

This is the electronic age, and businesses and consumers are converting their filing system from manual to electronic database. They are also saving and retrieving their data on and from the cloud, and from a company named Carbonite Information Center. However, I strongly recommend that hard copies of reports and customer documents be retained in a metal filing cabinet in case your computers are stolen or are out of commission, and customers happen to call the company on that day to place an order or to reconcile information on their accounts. Hard copies are excellent sources of backup for everything, including items that are difficult to back up, although with the advent of sophisticated scanners all documents are capable of scanning and saving on a computer's hard drive, flash drive, and CD indefinitely.

The trend is toward cloud computing as Internet-based software applications become more acceptable. Cloud application software is rapidly becoming a standard requirement and a necessity as more people and company employees use mobile devices and remote access software to store and retrieve information on the Internet.

If your company designs and sells products, then you would be required to hire designers, technicians, and/or engineers. Everybody in your technology department should learn from people in the sales, marketing, and accounting departments how the innovations and products they will create need to be sold. Hence, innovation, costs, and selling price must blend nicely into your product to attract buyers. I have seen many beautifully designed products get rejected by retail stores such as Walmart and Costco because the selling price of each product that was rejected was above the price the retailers would pay for them and then make a reasonable profit. Don't lose faith in your products if they are rejected by superstores such as Walmart and Costco. Selling is full of rejections, and your faith in your business and products will constantly be tested. They may not buy your products, but other stores will be happy to take your products on consignment and sell them at a higher margin, so shop around your products and keep an open mind.

International selling: International selling is a complex, multichannel, multicultural environment. Buyers used to rely upon sellers' salespeople to provide them with information. Today, advances in technology, growth of the Internet, and development of search engines have transformed markets and altered international selling because buyers and competitors have immediate access to company and industry information. As buyers' reliance upon their suppliers' salespeople as the primary provider of information continues to dissipate, choosing the best product to build or service to supply, and planning the best route to international sales, are becoming a science whereby only those companies that have the resources to navigate the complexities of international selling will become successful.

Modernize your website: The purpose of a website is to generate traffic and sales for a company through leads, clicks, and calls. However, if a new company needs funding and applies for loans or seeks venture capital, investors would log on and inspect the company's website to validate its business plan—to see if the business plan is a true representation of what the company is communicating online.

A website has to be in operation for several weeks, giving the major search engines time to crawl, pick it up, index it, optimize it, blog activity, and build links.

Your website should have photos of your products and services, and it should be able to take customers' orders and payments. Small-business owners should observe the 80:20 rule: 80 percent of your time was spent to set up your website system and social media connection, and you spent the remaining 20 percent of your time, or fifteen minutes per day, to connect with your social media group and/or modify the contents on your website and on your social media page.

Mobile devices: People carry cameras on their smart phones, and they are intrigued by what they can see, so give them a behind-the-scenes look at what is happening at your place of business, and they will send texts and post photos of your products and services to their community of friends and social media groups. Also, showcase yourself smiling, and if you have employees, showcase them too, and bring attention to the human aspect or side of your business.

Try to interact with customers from their smart phones. If you can get to interact with them online and sometimes in person, they would feel the emotional connection, like the attention they are getting, and become loyal, long-term customers.

It is important to respond to customers in a timely manner and with insightful information. How you answer questions, settle disputes, respond to compliments, and correct mistakes or errors can make or break your relationship with customers and their community of friends on social media.

Mobile applications: This software application is designed to operate on mobile devices such as iPhone, Android, BlackBerry, etc. Having a Mobile connection is a must for musicians and singers in the entertainment industry. Many musicians and singers have had their own custom-made mobile applications built specifically for their music. When the application is activated, it allows the artists' fans to listen to new songs and songs from their catalogue, view videos for new songs, view videos of concerts, tour dates, cities and countries, and other information that the artists want to share with fans around the world. Interactions with their fan base have helped the artists remain relevant with fans around the world, gain a lot of exposure, get more international listeners and a bigger fan base, more bookings, sellout tours, and huge merchandise sales.

Business planning: If you are planning to sell your products online, you will need a business plan and a strong strategic plan that would enable you to attract investors. This plan should help you as follows:

1. Stand out from the crowd
2. Generate sustainable sales
3. Generate strong gross margin
4. Generate free cash flow

You should do your homework by looking at business plans and related or associated documents from successful and failed companies. They can tell a lot about the strategies and assumptions (characteristics) of those companies. If you are familiar with the industry that they have operated in, then you can look at those documents and ask yourself some important questions and plan you strategies along those lines:

1. What are or what were the owner's core assumptions about the business?

_____

_____

_____

2. What were their assumptions about the size of the market?

_____

_____

_____

3. What were their assumptions about market growth?

_____

_____

_____

4. How did they plan to leverage the capabilities of the Internet?

_____

_____

_____

5. How did they plan to gain competitive advantage over traditional businesses?

_____

_____

_____

6. How did they plan to gain competitive advantage over established online competitors?

_____

_____

_____

7. What were their core strategies?

_____

_____

_____

Competition and market trends

A company is more likely to be outwitted by emerging competitors (new entrants) and new technologies than by its existing competitors. Eastman Kodak: Kodak was in the film business. Instead of listening to their customers and focusing on customers' need, management at Kodak wasted their time worrying about their closest competitor, **Fuji Films**. They did not foresee the long-term erosion of their market by **filmless cameras** that **Cannon** and **Sony** were bringing into the market. **Kodak** went into bankruptcy and receivership because management held tightly to old business methods when they should have been innovating to meet customers' demands. A lot of photography stores that had depended on Kodak have lost their businesses to Cannon, Sony, and new entrants in the new competitive environment. That can happen in any industry.

An Wang started Wang Laboratories in a rented room above a garage in Boston, USA. The company earned close to $15,000 in the first year of operation. Its products were an instant hit with large companies, and Wang Laboratories grew 35 percent per year. Its annual sales skyrocketed to $2 billion, and profits reached $200 million. Wang hardware and software were not compatible with those that were made by other companies. The company's proprietary strategy locked in customers and earned Wang high profit margins. Customers began asking for an "open system" that would have made Wang systems compatible with other systems. Wang became stubborn, refused to listen to them, and refused to change. Customers began migrating to other companies, and Wang eventually filed for bankruptcy. It emerged from bankruptcy one year later; but rapidly changing technology had made its computers obsolete (high-tech relics). The new CEO had to convince/persuade existing customers to remain with the company, transformed the company into a fast-paced consultancy service provider, and struggled to overcome the stigma or taint of bankruptcy.

Compaq computer was a success story. The company had carved out a niche with its high-margin, state of the art computers and had steady growth and great success for many years. **Samsung** and **Packard-Bell** entered the market with cheaper clones that were selling in discount stores and catalogs. In addition, **Samsung** and **Packard-Bell** were providing the same quality parts and sometimes higher quality parts faster and cheaper than those from Compaq's factory and its suppliers. Customers' preferences changed, and they started to buy the cheaper clones that were made by Samsung and Packard-Bell. **Compaq's** market had changed, and company executives were slow to react to the changes. Soon the company was on the verge of extinction. It rebounded after company executives reexamined consumers' needs and redefined the attributes that the company and its products must provide to consumers to regain its market share. Those changes are not unique to technology companies. Rather, they reflect fundamental changes in the way companies must design, build, and sell products as consumers' preferences and markets change.

Netflix saw the changing environment for movie delivery and survived the onslaught by bringing a service that changed the industry for rental movie delivery.

The banking industry saw the digital age coming, and they embraced the benefits of digital banking. They put in ATMs and brought out home banking. They took some losses through theft, but they were right on the heels of the issue, and in some cases were prepared for it.

JC Penny announced that it has plans to eliminate cash registers and checkout counters, replacing them with a patchwork of technology solutions, such as Wi-Fi networks, mobile checkout, and RFID (radio frequency identification) technology tracking systems for merchandise, as well as self-checkout options.

The advent and development of modern technology has enabled people to sit in the comfort of their homes and conduct business around the world. Some employers have capitalized on this modern trend, and they have allowed valuable employees who live in different time zones and rural or suburban areas, far away from their workplace, to work from home and commute to work less often, about one or two days per week or month. Working from home is sometimes referred to as telecommuting or working remotely.

This flexible work arrangement has enabled employees to have a "*work-life*" balance by moving out of their cubicles on the job and working in inspirational settings at home. This has increased employees' loyalty, maximized their time and productivity, and saved them and their employers money. Many employees have voted their company as: "The best company to work for." However, in 2013 this flexible work arrangement has gotten bad publicity as Yahoo CEO Marissa Mayer has stated her intention to eliminate the practice because she believes the workers have abused the privilege, and Best Buy stores are setting strict rules and policies to ensure that employees who are working from home are productive.

One employer in California who has twenty employees, five of whom work remotely, has told me he can use VPN logs on his computer server to track the productivity of those off-site workers. However, as a small company with a staff of tight-knit workers, he does not want to erode the trust that his workers have placed in the company. Hence, with input from his staff, his company has developed an effective tracking system that alerts everybody about who is actively working on what project.

Under the US tax code, an employee who has received permission to work from home instead of commuting to work daily and who must check in regularly with his or her employer via telephone, e-mail or conference call, and who is required to attend company meetings at least once a week or once monthly may qualify for the office-at-home deductions.

Take this challenge

Technology: Diana started a technology company in her bedroom and it has grown to serving 160,000 customers. Her workers received regular training, a salary, bonus, and other fringe benefits. A new competitor recruited or poached some of her best employees and began to erode her market share by offering and promising her customers more electronic features, lower prices, and better service. Diana knew her back was against the wall. She hired outside consultants and a private investigator to check whether her former employees had copied confidential information to external hard drives, sent e-mails with the information to her competitor, or claimed on their resumes that they had invented some of the stolen products and/or information. She also obtained information from the following sources:

1. Google search
2. Trade associations
3. Chambers of Commerce
4. Yellow Pages

She held conferences with her advisors and reliable customers, and she was told if her former employees had given confidential information to her competitor or stolen her intellectual property, proprietary products, or trade secrets and passed them on to her new competitor. If so, they could face imprisonment of up to ten years and pay a penalty of $250,000 each.

She had decided not to reduce her prices, so she focused instead on delivering higher quality customer service to compete against her new competitor. She reasoned that the cost of maintenance and replacement of technology equipment would be high for her new competitor, and she would regain market share in the long run when this competitor ran out of money and working capital and could not fulfill its promise to its employees and customers. If you were Diana's business partner or if you were a board member in a board meeting with Diana, what would be your advice to her and why?

_____

_____

_____

_____

CHAPTER 26
MARKETING, PRICING, AND SALES

1. Marketing

Companies and the industries that they operate in are exposed to market forces that sometimes make profitability difficult to sustain. They can certainly overcome those challenges by packaging their product and services appropriately. That is, they must bring together the right mix of products, customer service, prices, and discipline, and avoid getting involved in price wars.

Packaging

The packaging of your product or service is the image that you want to convey that would influence the purchasing decision of your target customers or target market. Packaging is a combination of the things that your customers see and the benefits they envisioned they will receive or the satisfaction they will enjoy when they purchase and use your product or service.

The total package includes the quality of your promotional items, such as wrapping paper, boxes, file folders, and shopping bags. The benefits or satisfaction includes product performance, user experience, return policy, guarantees, warrantees, and customer service experience. Please note that I did not mention anything about price because you are not competing on price. You are selling customer experience and customer satisfaction, which are the key issues that customers care about nowadays.

Price is a secondary issue. (Please read the paragraph about price in the chapter **"Product or Service."**)

Promotion

I am sure you are familiar with the proverb**: "The squeaking wheel gets the grease."** Your business may be producing the best product or service in the world, but you would not be able to sell it if nobody knows it exists. Marketing will create the awareness and demand for your products and services. Marketing is essential because for a business to thrive it must consistently attract sufficient customers to buy its products or services. Hence, your company must become good at marketing and set itself apart from its competitors in the marketplace. This method is called market differentiation.

Your first priority is to prepare a realistic marketing plan and have the resources to fund your marketing budget. Create awareness by marketing and promoting your business aggressively—online, in person, and within your community—and cultivate a customer base that would help you generate the necessary buzz for your company in the marketplace.

Every business has marketing costs, regardless if the business is involved with manufacturing, selling products, or selling services. Marketing costs include the following:

Controlling marketing costs

1. Advertising (print, signage/signs, billboards, TV, radio, and Internet)
2. Gifts and samples
3. Promotional items (business cards, brochures, calendars, books, shopping bags, etc.)

The marketing staff at Coca-Cola and the advertising agencies that Coca-Cola hired to craft its marketing campaign have taken their time to research customer attitudes and buying patterns; and they specifically design and produce culturally adapted promotions that resonate with their target audience in each of their four market regions.

The ability of the marketing people to link the company's logo and tagline—"The real thing"—to the cultural and aesthetic sensibilities of each group of targeted customers has won Coca-Cola customers' trust, differentiated the brand from its competitors, and enhanced its value and competitive advantage in the marketplace.

Coca Cola has four websites because it can afford to have them:

1. The regional site (**coca-cola.com**)
2. In China (**coca-cola.com.cn**)
3. In Germany (**coca-cola.de**)
4. In South Africa (**cocacola.co.za**)

Each website is culturally adapted and specifically designed to suit the sensibilities of a specific group of audiences in four regions. That is a brilliant move by Coca-Cola. However, paying to design four websites and paying a technical support staff to operate, manage, and maintain them is an expensive marketing concept or proposition for SMEs or small business owners, who need the cash to fund or finance their daily operating costs (working capital).

Here is what I have done to avoid high technology costs in my business. I serve clients in thirteen industries in the United States of America and overseas. I featured or showcased those industries on one website by having my technical people design a separate webpage for each industry. This technique has worked wonderfully for me. I am suggesting that small businesses try this money-saving, effective, and efficient technique. My website address is **ConsultantBarry.com.**

Differentiation is what you and your product or service do differently from everybody else's products or services. The only way to differentiate your product or service is by marketing its unique valuable qualities, such as:

(a) Its heritage
(b) Current customers' experience
(c) Market leadership in terms of present need
(d) Being first to emotionally connect customers to the product or service

This can only be accomplished by effective planning and skillful and timely execution of your advertising and marketing plan by your product, marketing, and sales staff with strong support from customer service and the credit and collections department.

Marketing budget: When you design a plan to market your product or service, you should have the necessary funds available to finance your budget. This may sound simplistic, but don't be surprised if you attend a business seminar and discover that there are people at the seminar who have drawn up their company's marketing budgets and did not have a clue where they would find or get the money to fund the budget and execute their plan.

2. Pricing

a. Pricing strategies: A business will not survive for long if it continues to operate at cost or below cost. The kind of pricing method you use would determine the kind of industry in which your business is operating. You may use a specific pricing method, or you can take parts from other pricing methods and create your own pricing method or system. Let your knowledge about your industry and your common sense guide you.

Here are some profitable pricing methods that are frequently used to sell products and services.

1. Penetration pricing
2. Fixed price
3. Loss leader pricing
4. Prestige pricing
5. ontingency fee
6. Fixed contract price
7. Bundle pricing
8. Discounting

b. Social status: Consumers in some countries consider products for domestic use, such as TVs, washing machines, and furniture as secondary products, and they would not be willing to pay high prices for them. Companies such as Best Buy, IKEA, and others have had to learn that the hard way and cut their prices by 30 percent to 50 percent. However, those same consumers will pay high prices for more visible, status-oriented products such as cars, jewelry, clothing, shoes, and bags that would help transform or elevate their social standings.

c. Managing prices: Don't go crazy cutting prices to get customers or to keep customers just because your competitors announced they are cutting prices. Cutting prices arbitrarily would reduce your **margin of safety** (see glossary). Instead, be realistic, and do your calculations and get a clear picture about whether your strategy to cut prices will pay off, or the impact price reduction will have on your profit margins over the long term.

3. Sales

Your company's sales and success will depend on the income size, needs, and spending patterns of your customer base. During a slow economy, demand for your product or service will fall as some of your customers lose their jobs and face budgetary constraints, and as competitors cut prices and become more aggressive to reduce overcapacity and to maintain or increase market share, working capital, and liquidity. To survive in this market, you must revise your company's business plan and focus on its strengths and its ability to generate additional revenue streams. You must execute your revised plan aggressively.

Pareto's principle: This principle, also known as the 80/20 rule, states that, for many events, roughly 80 percent of the effects come from 20 percent of the causes. Hence, in business, 80 percent of a company's sales will come from 20 percent of its customers. In business, the 80/20 rule is a rule of thumb that business managers follow and apply in their daily business operations. They use this principle to improve profitability by focusing on the most effective areas of their operations, and eliminating, automating, delegating, or retraining the rest of the organization as appropriate.

Sales forecast: A sales forecast should be prepared before a sales budget is prepared. A sales forecast is a projection of the following:

1. Estimated future sales in your industry $_____.
2. Estimated future sales of your company $_____.

The following factors should be considered when you are preparing the sales forecast for a specific budget period:

1. Sales from prior year $_____
2. Back orders $_____
3. Access and availability of supplies. How readily is supply available? _____

Sales budget: A sales budget is the key budget in the entire budgeting process, and business owners should prepare this budget first. It triggers a chain reaction that leads to the preparation and development of other budgets for your company. Sales budget can be used to direct and control sales efforts by:

1. Product
2. Customers
3. Territory
4. Salesperson

In a technology company, people in the Technology Department should learn how the innovations and products they will create need to be sold. Hence, they should work with the marketing, sales, credit, and accounting departments to ensure products they have designed and created can be sold when they are introduced to the market or landed in the market.

Sales costs are necessary in order to provide goods and services to customers—in order to get products or merchandise and services to customers. Sales costs a company will endure include the following:

1. Sales travel
2. Order costs (cost of obtaining or filling orders)
3. Handling and shipping
4. Sales salary
5. Sales commissions
6. Your business pricing policy, market share, and marketing plan

I appreciate feedback from my readers and clients. My e-mail address is **ClemBarry@ aol.com**, and my website is **www.ConsultantBarry.com**.

CHAPTER 27
DOING BUSINESS OVERSEAS

Thanks for buying my book. This bonus chapter is a token of my appreciation.

Please let me know how you are doing. Send me your comments. My e-mail is **ClemBarry@aol.com, and my** website is **www.ConsultantBarry.com**.

In her book *Ninety Percent of Everything*, Rose George, a British journalist and author, states: "It is less expensive to ship Scottish cod 10,000 miles away to China to be filleted and then sent back to Scotland than it is to pay Scottish workers to do the job. Of course, this reflects mostly on the cheapness of Chinese labor, but it does also show the low costs of shipping."

Those statements are bitter pills to swallow and I would not be surprised if those statements have angered the labor unions. Labor unions would despise the Scottish employers for outsourcing work to China. However, we are all aware that many companies generate most of their revenues selling their products overseas, making their products overseas, or outsourcing work to overseas companies. Here are some examples:

Land Rover is manufactured in the United Kingdom. Its new owner is Tata Motor Co, India, but its biggest sales and markets are in Brazil and China, not in the United Kingdom or India.

Japanese automobile manufacturers such as Toyota and Honda manufacture a lot of their automobiles and parts in the United States of America; and many of the American automobile manufacturers, such as GM, Ford, and Chrysler, manufacture a lot of their automobiles and parts in Canada, Mexico, and Brazil.

Agricultural products such as wheat, meat, and vegetables are enjoying record sales in the overseas markets while their sales are stagnant in local or domestic markets.

A well-known shoe company in Greece owned forty stores in the local market. It closed four stores there that were operating at a loss and opened eight new stores in Brazil and Argentina. Those stores are doing well over there, and the company has plans to open four more stores.

Many accounting and law firms are generating a lot of their revenue, if not most of their revenue, providing multicountry tax services for foreign corporations operating in the United States of America, expatriates working in other countries, and people with dual citizenship who must file tax returns and report their incomes in every country where they live and work. What we are experiencing in today's business climate is that local or domestic business owners must make their products and services available to overseas customers and clients if they want their businesses to thrive and become successful in the global economy.

Preparing for the overseas markets

Before you start doing business in other states, provinces, or countries, it is important that you boost your confidence by:

1. Reading everything that you can lay your hands on.
2. Talking to people who have done business in those states, provinces, or countries.
3. Talking to foreign coaches and foreign attachés.
4. Contacting people from those states, provinces, or countries whom you have met in school, seminars, conventions, trade shows, embassies, or foreign missions.
5. Finding out when your country will host an international trade show or trade fair. Rent a booth there, and give away samples of your products to foreign wholesalers, distributors, and tourists. Take their contact numbers and build a strategic partnership with them. Get feedback and small COD orders from them, and increase your market share slowly. Collect your money COD and by letter of credit through your bank. Don't get tempted into selling your product on consignment or open account unless you are a big company such as Johnson & Johnson.

6. Choosing those foreign countries that have lucrative markets for your products. Rent a booth at a trade show or trade fair in each country and give samples of your product to wholesalers and distributors and build strategic partnerships. Get feedback and small COD orders from them, and increase your market share slowly. If your market share continues to increase rapidly, be prepared to face allegations of **"dumping"** and **antitrust laws.**

Transatlantic Trade and Investment Partnership

In February 2013 the United States and the European Union announced the beginning of negotiations of the Transatlantic Trade and Investment Partnership. The transatlantic trade relation is the backbone of the world economy. The European Union and the United States of America account for over one third of the global trade flows and about 45 percent of the world GDP. The declared purpose of the agreement is to get as close as possible to eliminating all duties on transatlantic trade in industrial and agricultural products, with a special treatment for the most sensitive products. Negotiations will aim to achieve ambitious outcomes in:

1. Trade regulation issues
2. Removal of tariffs and nontariff barriers
3. Access to markets
4. Principles and new modes of cooperation to address shared global trade challenges and opportunities.

The most significant trade barrier is the so-called "behind-the-border" obstacles to trade, such as the different safety and environmental standards for automobiles. Presently, merchants or traders who want to sell their products in both Europe and the United States of America must pay duty twice and comply twice with procedures to get their products approved. The goal of this trade negotiation is to reduce unnecessary costs and delays for companies or traders while maintaining environmental safety and protection.

According to the European Commission memo, the commercial treaty could generate up to 86 billion euros for the European Union and 65 billion euros for the United States of America.

Patents and trademarks

Refrain from doing business overseas until you have the right overseas protection. If your product is patented and trademarked in the United States of America, you may not have protection selling it overseas. In the United States of America, if two persons apply for a patent for the same idea, the person who is **approved first** gets the patent. However, in many countries the applicant who **files first** gets the patent. Also, many countries would not grant you a patent if you had started selling your products over there without having their patent approval.

In November 2005, the United States of America joined the Madrid Protocol. The US membership allows US companies to file for trademark protection in sixty countries simultaneously. The Patent Corporation Treaty (PCT) signed by 120 countries could also help you. If you file for protection under the PCT within one year after you filed your patent in the United States of America, you will be allowed an additional eighteen months to file for your patent in any of the other signatory countries, even if you are already selling your product or service over there.

Investor visa or economic citizenship

The United Kingdom, United States of America, Canada, Austria, and several small and large countries make this visa or citizenship program available to foreign investors. This is a booming business in many countries. The demand is so great in Canada that the government has stopped accepting new applications. Approval in some countries is quick and can take up to ninety days. Approved applicants can donate a fixed amount of money to a special charitable fund or invest a prescribed amount of money in a real estate project, designated economically depressed area, or a business that employs a specified number of workers and get a passport.

Establishing channels of distributions

Business owners usually encounter problems overseas because of the scant knowledge they have about transacting business overseas or operating a business in a foreign country. As a business owner, you should consider spending most of your time working with qualified prospects. Your time is too limited and too valuable for you to be chasing after dead-end leads and prospects that are struggling to make purchasing decisions. Therefore, it is imperative that you find and hire the right people to represent your business.

1. **Freight forwarders** are important for their expertise in export details and strategies, to prepare your shipping or export documents; to arrange for inland freight, packaging, and warehousing; to select the appropriate ocean or air carrier, freight, and insurance coverage; to follow the fate of the shipment in transit and at the final destination; and to file transportation and insurance claims for damages and losses of the shipment or part thereof. However, a small manufacturer who is shipping one pallet of product to an overseas customer or consignee and wants to remain in control of the collections and claims processes can hire a freight forwarder to prepare the shipping documents. The manufacturer or consignor would take those documents and other documents that are pertinent to the transaction to a local commercial bank with instructions to forward them to the customer's or consignee's bank overseas.

2. **Overseas distributors** are important for their knowledge of foreign importation requirements and for their ability to take title of the goods as soon as they are landed in the port and for quick entry to the market. Establish realistic goals that both of you can accomplish together and draw up a contract that is clear and equitable to both of you. The spirit of clear and mutual cooperation will determine the overall success of the product. If you or the distributors must regularly refer to stipulations in the contract, then the relationship is in trouble.

Oftentimes, people will bypass your overseas representatives and want to do business directly with you. In situations like that it would be wise for you to prequalify them quickly by asking them questions from a written list that you have prepared for those occasions. If they have the authority to make purchasing decisions and meet your other requirements, then you can accept their purchase orders and credit card information or a letter of credit, if doing so will not jeopardize the relationship between yourself and your wholesalers and distributors.

Selling overseas

Some entrepreneurs have told me it is important for their companies to expand overseas. A Chinese businessman told me when he started his business in China, his inability to secure a market overseas had put his company at a disadvantage because operating in overseas markets, such as in the United States of America, generally means better profits, whereas in China his company has to compete for a small margin of profit (margin-killing competition). He said his company and product were present in China and not overseas, so they were considered regional brands and not global brands. Also, success overseas means recognition by Chinese consumers. If his company or products do well overseas, that success will make his brand more valuable among Chinese consumers. If you have a similar story, please share it with me.

Planning

Your business plan and your method of operation would set the course for the goals that you want to accomplish for your business. If you have plans to sell your product or service overseas and become successful doing business abroad, you should select countries that have attractive markets for your products and services, and you should review the trade treaty that your country has with those countries. You should be aware of foreign governments' plans to boost their local economies. In addition, your ability to interact and relate to people of various cultures and customs is crucial if you do not have an overseas representative to help you conduct your trade. Here are other factors that you must take into consideration during your planning process:

1. Which product or service do you believe your company can sell quickly in foreign markets?
2. What needs would your product or service fulfill in the overseas market?
3. Do you have sufficient data about the demographics of the population, the size of their disposable incomes, and their buying patterns?
4. How about currency control and availability and stability of exchange rates?
5. What are your selling terms? Why?
6. What are the selling terms of your competitors? Why?
7. How much do you plan to sell in the short term?
8. How much do you plan to sell in the long term?

9. How competitive is your product or service in the foreign markets?

10. What are the similarities and differences between the domestic and foreign markets?

11. Are you prepared to give your overseas customers the same level of dedicated services that you give to your local or domestic customers?

12. Are overseas intermediaries available to help you? What are their terms and conditions?

13. Are overseas distributors interested in selling your products? If so, what are their terms and conditions?

14. Are you willing to commit resources of time, people, and finance to your overseas program? How much do you plan to commit?

15. Are you complying with "dumping" laws? Dumping is the term used when a product that was manufactured in one country is shipped to another country, and it is selling over there for less than the price in the domestic market, or it is selling over there at below the cost to produce it.

Freight forwarders are an integral part of the exporting business. Virtually all shippers depend on them for varying degrees of service. They are regulated and certified by the FMC, which regularly audits them to ensure they follow the rules for licensing and bonding.

Manufacturing overseas

Sun Mark, UK, could be described as a "rags to riches" story that shows the benefits of hard work. Rami Ranger, owner and founder of Sun Mark, UK, a manufacturer of its own line of products and a global distributor for some of the United Kingdom's most established and well-known food brands, started the business from a rented shed with start-up capital of just £2 (⬜2.40) and a £40 (⬜48) typewriter. The company has had to overcome HMS customs rigorous or stringent clearance rules and regulations to carve out a niche for itself in the overseas markets. Seventeen years later, the key to its global success is the excellent quality of its services and products coupled with competitive prices.

Knowledge of local customs and tastes in individual markets overseas has played a vital role in the company's growth in other countries. An important part of Sun Mark's success is that it is the only British company to have gained three consecutive Queen's Awards for "Enterprise in International Trade."

When asked what advice he has for entrepreneurs, Ranger said: "It is always wise not to put all your eggs in one basket. Similarly, it is wise to do business in as many countries as possible in order to insulate your business from economic turmoil and political unrest in a particular country. Sun Mark has strongly diversified its international business, and today distributes its foods across Europe and to Africa, Asia, the Americas, and the Middle East."

If you have plans to manufacture your products overseas and sell your finished products in foreign markets or ship them back home to your local or domestic market, you should review the overseas governments' plans to stimulate economic growth opportunities for local manufacturers and incentives or concessions they are offering foreign investors. In addition, you should seriously take into consideration the following factors that are sometimes overlooked by foreign manufactures:

1. The size, quality, and work ethic of the overseas workforce
2. Trade agreements (nontariff products, tax treaties, quotas, permits, licenses, stability of foreign exchange rate, and repatriation of income laws)
3. Labor cost and labor and employment laws
4. The frequency of strikes and civil unrests
5. Communication and transportation infrastructural development
6. The cost and stability of energy, power, or electricity
7. Shipping distances
8. Availability of raw materials
9. The availability of natural resources
10. The ability of overseas partners and intermediaries to get things done quickly
11. Transfer pricing and value-added tax (VAT)

Business acquisition overseas

You are focusing primarily on existing overseas markets, but you won't miss an opportunity to make an important acquisition overseas if the US dollars that your company was hoarding in its bank accounts began to lose value and purchasing power. Hence, in May 2013 the Chinese company **Shuanghui International Holdings Ltd.**, China's largest meat processing company, agreed to buy the world's biggest pork producer, Virginia-based **Smithfield Foods**, for approximately $4.72 billion plus debt acquisition of $2.38 billion for a total of value of $7.1 billion. Smithfield's brands include Armour, Farmland, and Smithfield.

In March 2013, thirteen thousand dead pigs were found floating in a river in China. Two months later, in May 2013, a Chinese company acquired the biggest pork producer and processor in the United States of America. Is that a coincidence, or a smart business practice by the Chinese? I believe China's growing middle class is prepared to pay a premium for pork. This was also a smart way for the Chinese to quickly get rid of billions of dollars in their company's business accounts that continue to depreciate in value in exchange for a great asset, Smithfield pork brands, which are in high demand in China.

International taxation

For US expatriates (expats) living abroad and for foreign nationals living in or doing business in the United States of America, the tax preparation process begins with an in-person consultation, especially for those clients who are new to the US reporting system.

1. US individuals working abroad, foreign taxpayers with US income, foreign bank accounts of US persons, report of foreign bank and financial accounts, treaty-based return position disclosure—IRC 6114 or 7701(b)—US expatriates around the world, and UK expatriates in the United States of America are liable—tax returns are due every year by April 15.
2. US exporters, US partnerships with foreign owners, and US subsidiaries of foreign parents are liable—tax returns are due every year by April 15.
3. A foreign corporation doing business in the United States of America must file a US tax return every year whether or not it had income or a permanent establishment in the United States of America. The return is due two and a half months after the close of the tax year.
4. A US corporation doing business overseas must file a US tax return every year whether or not it had income. The return is due two and a half months after the close of the tax year.

5. Tax evasion is high on the EU agenda, as EU members accused Ireland of being a tax haven for multinational corporations that allegedly swindled over $1 trillion in taxes from EU member states. Policy officials at Transparency International are pushing the European Union to force foreign corporations to produce and share detailed financial and fiscal information about the income they earn and the taxes they pay in every country where they operate. This follows allegations and suspicion about the way foreign corporations such as Apple, Google, Amazon, and Starbucks handle their tax affairs.

The whistle-blower act

1. The SEC Program

Over the past five years, several countries have passed new laws or strengthened existing laws to protect whistle-blowers. In the United States of America, the "Whistleblower Protection Enhancement Act of 2012" is administered by the Securities and Exchange Commission (SEC). It was enacted to encourage, reward, and protect employees at financial institutions for reporting suspicions of wrongdoing or fraud inside their companies after they have reported their concerns to their employers. This was evidence during the accounting and financial scandal that led to the collapse of several major corporations, notably Enron, WorldCom, and Arthur Anderson, after which Congress passed the Sarbanes-Oxley Act in 2002, holding the CEO and CFO accountable and criminally liable for fraudulent financial reporting acts or financial shenanigans at their companies. One hundred and sixty-four complaints were filed under this act.

Passage of the Dodd-Frank Act in 2010 has extended the whistle-blower act to the private sector. This program is also administered by the Securities and Exchange Commission (SEC).Whistle-blowers can collect 15 to 30 percent of any fine that exceeds $1 million that a company must pay as a result of the whistle-blower's original information and voluntary cooperation. Employees who have suffered a backlash from their employers in retaliation for snitching on them can pursue claims against their employers in federal court.

When the law was first enacted in 2012, the SEC reported that a total of 3,001 whistle-blower complaints were filed. This includes 2,507 complaints from workers in the United

States of America. The SEC paid out 10 percent of the budgeted $452 million that it had allocated for paying rewards. The SEC does not reward informants who were part of the original fraud. Tips came from all fifty states, the District of Columbia, and Puerto Rico, and from forty-nine foreign countries. Among those foreign countries, the United Kingdom, Canada, and India filed the most complaints. Complaints range from:

1. Corporations' financial disclosure (18 percent)
2. Fraud (15 percent)
3. Financial manipulation (15 percent)

2. The IRS program

The Internal Revenue Service has a similar whistle-blowers program like the one that is administered by the SEC. However, the IRS will pay whistle-blowers who have participated in the crime. In September 2012, the IRS paid $104 million to a former UBS banker who gave information in which UBS Bank and the former banker helped wealthy clients hide money from the US government. The information has helped the US Treasury collect $780 million in fines from UBS Bank. However, the former employee spent thirty months in prison before receiving the $104 million because it was alleged he had withheld pertinent information from US Treasury investigators.

Courtesy: If you plan to do business overseas, it is important that you show respect to your hosts by having breakfast or dinner with them. If you refuse to do so, or if you attend and refuse to eat because you dislike the preparation of certain meats or dishes, then that is a mark of disrespect, and you have embarrassed your host and damaged a potential good relationship. Sampling every dish that was presented on the table shows that you have respect for your hosts. In some Asian and European countries, it is common courtesy, and it is legal, for clients to present gifts to contractors, accountants, lawyers, etc. It is disrespectful if you refused to accept gifts from your clients. However, **that same gratitude may be considered illegal (bribery) in some Western countries**.

The Foreign Corrupt Practices Act (FCPA): This is a federal law that was enacted in 1977. It prohibits US companies and individuals from paying bribes to foreign government officials, political figures, etc., for the purpose of obtaining business. Punishments allowable under the act include fines of up to twice the amount of benefit an individual is expected to receive from the bribery. In addition, that person can face up to five years imprisonment. The act covers a variety of antibribery and accounting topics and provisions, including who and what is covered by FCPA, the definition of a "foreign official," what constitutes proper and improper gifts, travel and entertainment expenses, the nature of facilitating payments, how successor liability applies in the mergers and acquisitions context, the hallmarks of an effective corporate compliance program, and the different types of civil and criminal resolutions available in the FCPA context.

Currency fluctuations: In October 2012, the BBC reported that McDonald's had reported a worse than expected third quarter profit due to the strong US dollar and increasing competition. Hence, currency fluctuations can make your company sales worth more or less when your profits are repatriated. If your main business (parent company) is located in the United States of America or the United Kingdom, a strong dollar or pound means your overseas sales are worth less, and your profit will worth less when it is repatriated to you back in those two countries. In addition, you have to pay corporation taxes on the profit. Therefore, your company would retain less money to pay dividends to its shareholders. If shareholders are not happy with the return on their investments, they will get angry and sell or "dump" the shares of stock in your company. That is one of the reasons why some American companies are lobbying the US Congress to reduce the tax rate on corporate profit. Some of them have moved their headquarters and intellectual property (copyrights, patents, etc.) to other countries, such as Ireland, where they have received government concessions and a corporate tax rate on profits that is 50 percent lower than their native United States of America.

Payment (letter of credit and bank drafts): A letter of credit is a safe way for collecting payment from overseas consignees. A letter of credit should be used by the seller if the seller plans to ship merchandise to a consignee for more than a year. It is used to establish long business transactions. Letters of credit are usually not used for shipment by air because the merchandise will arrive quickly and incur storage/demurrage charges at the airport while the letter of credit document can take several weeks to arrive before the shipment can be cleared.

Use letters of credit for all overseas customers with whom you do not have a history. Ensure everything in the letter of credit is set up the way you want it at the beginning of the process, and request that a draft of the letter of credit be sent to you.

When you, the consignor, fill out the terms of the letter of credit, it becomes the responsibility of the customer's or consignee's bank (opening bank) to pay you, because it had secured the letter of credit. Hence, before the merchandise is shipped, you should discuss with your customer what you will ship and the terms and conditions, and incorporate them in the letter of credit.

Culture: Understanding the personal need, desires, goals, and nature of all job applicants and employees is critical to the success of your business. Everybody who is contemplating opening a business in a foreign country should understand the socioeconomic and sociopolitical culture or nature of that country. People are very sensitive in areas such as religion, culture, ethnicity, and politics. The nature and content of what you say could trigger protests, demonstrations, or boycott of your product. **What you say may be factual and intelligent to reasonable people, but it may be wrong and disrespectful to others because it was not the politically correct thing to say**. If your comment was too sensitive, then you will have to take the heat or blame for being too insensitive.

Labor unions

KFC Nepal faces closure

ZEE New .COM, Friday, August 17, 2012

KFC restaurants in Nepal, opened here with Indian investment, face closure after Maoist trade union activists attacked and threatened to kill senior managers, a company official said on Friday. Some Maoist trade union activists have beaten up and threatened the management staff of the company and even interfered with their works like hiring and transferring of staff, senior management of the company told PTI on condition of anonymity.

"The KFC restaurants may be permanently closed down if the situation does not improve," the management staff said. "We are open for dialogue but the trade union has not yet come up for negotiations," said the senior staff.

The fate of around 180 local employees working at the KFC and Pizza Hut is hanging in the balance after the international chain of restaurants shut down indefinitely. In the past, many Indian investors had to face similar labor unrest in Nepal. Surya Nepal, a joint venture of Indian Tobacco Company, had closed down its garment manufacturing unit situated in southern Nepal last year following continued labor unrest. A similar type of labor problem was faced by UniLiver, another multinational company with Indian investors. Colgate Palmolive permanently shut down its operation a couple of years ago.

Partner(s): In some countries you may be required to enter into a partnership agreement with a local individual or individuals as a requirement for doing business there. Your company will receive tax incentives to start and grow its business, and they don't want you to skip town and take all the profits with you. Some of the profits must remain in the country. Some countries may not specify that requirement. However, people who have tried to operate businesses in foreign countries without having a foreign partner on board have learned some very unpleasant lessons. They had scant knowledge about operating business overseas, and although they had hired local advisers in those countries, those advisers did not have what it would take to get things done. A foreign partner usually has the business experience, finances, connections, and the knowledge to connect your brand to local consumers.

Security deposit: Some foreign countries may require your company to put into escrow a security deposit or bond ($50,000 or more) that they would cash and use to pay liabilities such as payroll and your company's portion of the National Insurance Contribution (NIC), severance pay, and other contingent liabilities that you and your company are required to pay if you close your business and go back to your country.

Rent: If space is available in the designated busy shopping areas, and you choose to open your business there, the landlord may require that your company pay one year of rent in advance. Some landlords may require that you pay two years or three years of rent in advance. They will then turn around and give you a few months of free rent while you renovate the premises. In either case, you will have to guarantee the payment of the balance of the rent on your company's lease, and you must pay the monthly rent on time. Hence, if you bank with a US bank, you will have to take your lease to the branch in that foreign country and get a **letter of guarantee** that the balance of the money that you and your company owe on the lease is secured in escrow. **In foreign parlance that means:**

1. **"The landlord does not want you to close your company and leave him holding on to an empty bag."**
2. **"The landlord doesn't want you to leave him hanging high and dry."**

Some people have used a letter of credit (LC) instead of cash security deposit to secure the balance of money their company owed for commercial leased space. The letter of credit frees up cash and makes it available for working capital.

Permits: Beware that some countries prefer to do business with big foreign businesses—foreign direct investments. Sometimes small-business applicants would have to wait for three years before those countries would approve their business applications or grant them a permit or license. Reports have shown that some countries, such as Greece, Brazil, and the United Kingdom are changing their rules to speed up business registrations and licensing approvals in order to generate revenue and manage the underground economy more effectively.

Energy: High electricity and fuel costs can put your company's products at a disadvantage against imported products. Before you open your business overseas or abroad, and during the time that you are doing your feasibility study (evaluating the cost and benefit of starting or buying a business), ensure that the country has a stable supply of electricity. In some developing countries, power supply is shut off for several hours during the day, and business owners are required to provide their own source of power supply. Hence, you may be required to have a backup generator or pay your landlord an additional amount of money to provide your company with private electricity. Pay close attention to the cost of energy, and budget appropriately. In many countries, businesses that have failed have blamed the high cost of electricity as one of the primary reasons for their demise. Private citizens are enjoying free electricity. They are paying electricians to steal electricity from the main power supply, and the cost of the electricity to the power station is passed on to the business owners. Hence, that and many other unforeseen costs have driven many businesses out of many developing countries.

Concessions and subsidies: Governments around the world are offering tax concessions and other incentives, including economic citizenship, to encourage foreign business owners and investors to invest in their countries. This is commonly referred to as **"Attracting foreign direct investments (FDIs)."**

If you are planning to expand your business overseas, the offerings or the impressive developmental aids that would be given to you could motivate you to move there quicker. However, it is important that you keep a cool head and carefully analyze the business investment climate in those countries:

1. Investor friendly regulations.

    a. Are the business and trade policies recently overhauled? Are they complex or simplified?

    b. How quickly do they process and approve business applications and licenses?

    c. Are the regulatory oversights necessary and cost-effective to the business?

    d. Are the regulatory oversights unreasonable and burdensome?

    e. Are concessions, subsidies, and incentives available?

    f. Would the country be able to provide those concessions and incentives in the long run?

2. What do governments and stakeholders expect in return for concessions and incentives they give to foreign investors?

In October 2012, there was a massive and violent strike at the Lonmin's Platinum Mine in Marikina, near Rustenburg, in South Africa. The miners complained that the mine owners had received funding from one of the international lending organizations with a stipulation attached to develop the local community. They claimed the owners had reneged on the stipulation in the contract, and they had abdicated their responsibilities, and that had caused miners to be living in deplorable conditions in rented tin shacks that surround the mines, and there continued to be prolonged problems with their wages, housing, health, unemployment, and the environment. They felt they were marginalized, and their only alternative was to fight for social justice and human dignity.

3. Political, social, and fiscal stability.

    a. Human rights

    b. Transparency and accountability (contracts/bids/tenders and procurement)

    c. Currency stability (stabilization)

Here we are concerned about the country's strategic planning, balanced budgets, relationships with credit rating and regulatory agencies such as Standard & Poor's, FITCH, and financial/lending institutions such as the IMF, World Bank, Caribbean Development Bank, Inter-American Development Bank, ECB, etc.

Beware of countries that do not have an efficient and effective method for collecting tax revenues. That can lead to the accumulation of uncollected tax revenues and a hike in the tax rates to balance new budgets. Similarly, a lack of transparency and accountability for awarding or tending contracts and procurement of contracts are indications of mismanagement and poor governance. That should convey to investors that the government in that country is not committed to promoting efficiency and reduction in waste, abuse, fraud, and corruption.

Poor governance is a turnoff for lending and regulatory institutions, and they are happy to recommend economic reforms and institute austerity measures. There would also be protests and violent demonstrations from citizens who felt new taxes were unfairly imposed on them to fill budget gaps. Many of us have witnessed the violent protests of citizens in the United Kingdom and other EU member states.

Those upheavals have scared away prospective investors; hurt the tourism industry; reduced the flow of foreign currency into the country; reduced the GDP, balance of trade, and payment of the country; and caused an increase in insurance premiums. Those are additional costs that must be passed on to consumers in the form of higher prices in an economic recession.

I know a store owner who used to sell one item for $50 and had to change his selling strategy to enable his business to survive. He is charging the same $50 for selling two or more of the same items.

Increased costs, riots, and economic recessions are deadly combinations. Before you invest, listen carefully and evaluate information from the natives in the country in which you are operating. They know more about their country than you do.

4. Foreign tax treaties (especially those tax treaties with your country).

5. Economic condition of the country and the community where your business will be located. This includes:

    a. Infrastructural and environmental development (hotels, manufacturers, and retailers are concerned about reliable and predictable energy supplies and costs, and about a modern communication system to enable them to compete effectively. High energy costs make local manufactured products more expensive than imported products. Unreliable and high costs of energy supply have driven a lot of companies out of business.

    b. The demographics of the population.

    c. Consumer preferences (lifestyle, spending patterns, and preferred shopping days).

    d. The availability of skilled labor (the number of skilled workers and the work ethic of the workforce).

6. The unemployment rate.

7. The crime rate (a high crime rate and corruption will deter economic development, and that is counterproductive to operating a profitable business.

8. Labor laws:

    a. Operating hours and days

    b. Labor rates, pay period (weekly/monthly)

    c. Employer contributions

    d. Number of paid vacation days

    e. Number of government holidays during the year

    f. Labor unions and their power and history of negotiations or bargaining during business reforms and downsizing.

If you are a professional golfer, race car driver, race horse owner, etc. (sports tourism), and you can encourage your peers and their superfans around the world to join your tournaments in a developing country, then you can negotiate a land deal with the government to build a golf course, car race track, horse race track, or sports training center. Many stars and superstars have gotten those deals because they are creating employment and boosting the tourism trade and the economies in those countries. If you are in the hospitality industry, and you are catering to international clients (tourism), and you want to build a hotel or casino in a developing country, you can negotiate with the government for tax concessions because you are catering to the superfans and colleagues of sports and entertainment superstars (discussed above), and the airlines, yachts, and passenger ships that brought them into the country where they will spend their money.

If you are a manufacturer, and you are manufacturing products or producing heavy equipment, machines, and automobile to ship overseas, you can negotiate with the government for tax concessions. You are providing employment for the citizens and boosting export and foreign exchange earnings for those countries. You are also helping the tourism industry in that country because your sales representatives, investors or shareholders, customers, suppliers, friends, and members of your trade or profession from abroad or overseas will be visiting your plant from time to time.

Some countries may award your company duty-free concessions (tax exemption) for machinery and equipment that you imported into the country to start or operate your business if similar machines and equipment are not sold or manufactured in that country. If similar machinery and equipment are sold or manufactured in that country, you are required to buy them from the distributors or manufacturers. Money from those sales help to create a vibrant economy—create jobs, reduce unemployment, pay VAT or sales tax to the Inland Revenue Department (Treasury), and reduce the balance of payment. If you don't buy the machinery and equipment locally, then the customs department in that country would levy a high import tax on you that would make importing more expensive than buying local—to deter you from buying outside of the country. However, Chinese manufacturers would not sit idle and watch other manufacturers (foreign or domestic) put them out of business, so they have devised a loophole: You can give the Chinese manufacturer the total estimated cost that the machinery and equipment would cost you if you purchased them locally. The manufacturer will ship you the same machinery and equipment at a lower price so that when the import duty in your country is added to the cost, your total cost would still be lower than the price you would have paid if you had purchased them at home.

If you want to start a business in one of the Caribbean islands, or a country in Africa or Europe, check with the Consulate Office in New York; Washington, DC; or the United Kingdom; or locate one of their offices in your country. Almost every country is offering incentives to encourage local and foreign investors to start new businesses, create jobs for the backlog of unemployed workers (14 percent to 24 percent unemployed), and generate revenue for the treasury or revenue department.

I appreciate feedback from my readers and clients. My e-mail address is **ClemBarry@ aol.com**, and my website is **www.ConsultantBarry.com**.

CHAPTER 28

PERSONAL COACH/ MENTOR PROGRAM

A coach helps the client take the necessary steps to get to where the client wants to be. The client comes to the relationship with a goal about what he/she wants to achieve but not knowing the steps to take to reach that goal.

A mentor is more like a teacher-student relationship. A mentor is a facilitator for the process required to help clients achieve their goals. A mentor teaches from a repertoire of experiences, knowledge, and insights that she or he has learned firsthand.

Stop making excuses; "Make money!"

Your competitors will not sit around waiting for you to figure out if you want to remain in business. They will capitalize on your mistakes/complacency, gobble up your market share, and put you out of business. These facts also hold true if you have plans to start a business and make it profitable. You have to come out with a "bang"—the *wow* factor. You need to have plans that will help you to hit the ground running, and you need to keep the momentum flowing. You are either in business or out of business. This is the reality of the business world/globalization.

Questions from clients

1. **"I started an ad agency in my home to supplement my $45,000 salary. My hobby had gross income of $72,000 last year. I received a promotion on my**

job, and my new salary is $60,000 plus benefits. My new position demands more of my time, but I do not want to deceive the clients I worked so hard to attain. I may need them if I get fired from my job. I am at a crossroad. What should I do?"

2. "I started a hobby and later turned it into a business. The business flopped, and I lost about $25,000 of start-up costs. I can't figure out what I did wrong. Do you have any suggestions?"

3. "I have owned and operated a small, profitable business for several years. I am often criticized for keeping the business small. I have done some research, and I realized some large businesses are doing very well. Some have emerged from bankruptcy, and some are heading for bankruptcy. Some of my critics do not have a clue about what it takes to run a profitable business. Should my business remain small, flexible, and profitable, or should I listen to some of my critics and expand?"

4. "I have been working as an employee for over twelve years. I have some money that I would like to use to buy or start a business. I have been warned that working as an employee for a large corporation is different from business ownership or entrepreneurship. I have never owned a business, and I do not want to make costly mistakes. Could you help me achieve the same level of business success that you have helped your clients/students achieve?"

Jump ahead of your competitors

My personal coach/mentor program was started in 2004, and a lot of people have benefited from it.

It is a one-on-one training session: If you wish to participate in a one-on-one session with a mentor, my personal coach program will help you to clarify your goals and focus on your objectives. **My one-on-one mentor/coaching program** is the best accelerated and comprehensive program on the market for people who do not have time to waste.

The session is customized to meet your specific needs, and you will receive a training manual. At the end of the training session, all trainees receive unlimited support and objective feedback for as long as they have the need for them, and

at no extra cost to them. They can call me Monday through Friday from 11:00 a.m. to 4:00 p.m. with related questions and obtain step-by-step practical solutions to quickly resolve their business problems **Trainees have discovered the difference between being a great professional or tradesman and operating a profitable and successful business.**

Coaching sessions are available annually during the months of May to December. Each session begins ten days after a trainee and I have discussed his/her goals, strengths, and weaknesses, and the trainee has signed the agreement and paid the fee. Each session may last for one or two days.

Bonus discussions

"A business or practice was very busy throughout the year, but it was deemed not profitable at the end of the year, and the bank refused to extend its credit line."

I will tell you the traditional and forensic side of this equation. You will learn how to avoid this dilemma in your practice or business when you become my student. This bonus discussion has earned me thousands of dollars in consultation fees and saved my clients thousands of dollars in lost revenues. I am giving it to you **FREE**.

Testimonials

"Your mentor program is great. I moved to Miami and purchased the business of my dreams nine months later. I am planning to open another store in the fall just like you predicted; and I am counting on your support."
—*Angelina Cruz, retailer, Miami, Florida*

"I opened my second store to accommodate upscale shoppers, and my collections are flying off the racks. I am ready to franchise my brand, and I have plans to take the business public. Thanks for believing in me, and thanks for being there for me."
—*Angelina Cruz, retailer, Miami, Florida*

"I used the ideas you recommended in your personal coach (mentor) program, and *wow*! My phone was ringing nonstop. My profit has doubled in one year. Joycelyn told

me she has achieved similar results in her second year, and she has plans to open an office in my county. Please do not coach anybody else in my county. I want my competitors to work their brains out competing against me. You are a good man, Barry."
—*Henry Alexis, tax preparer, Fort Lauderdale, Florida*

"The businesses we inherited were in total disarray. Barry helped us reorganize them and turn them around. The training and support services we received were terrific. The business cash flow has improved tremendously, and we are not paying any bank fees. Our suppliers have become more reliable, and the banks have increased our revolving line of credit."
—**Andre, Julian, and Mindy Roache, store owners, Brooklyn and Queens, New York**

COACHING REQUEST FORM

"Setting achievable goals and developing action plans"

Coach name: Dr. Clemson (Clem) Barry

**Tel # (718) 677-4006; e-mail: ClemBarry@aol.com;
website: www.ConsultantBarry.com**

Check one box: **[ ] One-day accelerated coaching**
[ ] Two-day accelerated coaching
[ ] Coaching every month for four months

Your Name _____ Cell # _____

Best time to call _____ E-mail _____

Business Name _____ Tel # _____

What industry are you interested in? _____

What progress, success, or breakthrough have you had in this industry?
_____
_____

What have you avoided, come up against, or struggling to resolve?
_____
_____

What do you expect to achieve at the end of the session?
_____
_____

How soon do you plan to start the session? _____

**PLEASE NOTE: Sessions will be customized to meet your needs, and you will
receive a training manual. At the end of the session you will receive unlimited
support and objective feedback at no extra cost to you.**

GLOSSARY

absorption costing: A managerial accounting method that includes all costs that are associated with manufacturing a product. It is a method used to price a product in which all fixed and variable costs that are associated in producing the product are allocated or apportioned to cost centers that are economically involved in producing the product.

account: A record of monetary transactions; a record of events.

accountable: To be held liable or responsible.

accountancy: The profession or duty of an accountant.

accountant: A person who is skilled in accounting; one whose job is to keep or inspect financial accounts.

accounting: The system of classifying, recording, and summarizing business and financial transactions.

aging of accounts receivable: Analyzing customers' accounts by the number of days they have been unpaid on the books.

allocation: Assigning various items of cost or revenue to segments of an organization according to a common cause, benefits received, or other rational measure of use.

antitrust legislation: It is sometimes referred to as "competition laws." It is intended to promote free competition in the marketplace by outlawing monopolies. This law was enacted by Congress to outlaw or restrict business practices that are considered to be monopolistic and restrain interstate commerce.

assess: To be charged with a tax, fine, or other payment.

assets: The value of everything that a business or person owns.

asset method of valuation: This is one of several methods used to value a business. It is the total value of what the business owns less/minus its total debts to creditors. It is sometimes referred to as the **"liquidated value"** of the business.

back taxes: Taxes owed from a previous year or from previous years.

balance sheet: A financial statement that shows what assets a company owns and how those assets are financed in the form of liabilities and ownership interest.

break-even point: The point of business activity where total revenue and total expenses are equal.

bookkeeping: The activity of keeping records of the financial affairs of a business.

budget: A financial plan/projection to estimate the results of future operations or capital projects.

budget variance: The difference between an actual and a budget amount.

business consultant: A person who is thorough about general business operations, or well versed in the operations of a specific industry.

business ethics: A system of morals; standards of behavior or belief; principles that govern business behavior; what is right and prudent with reference to a trade, business, or profession.

business purpose: The business reason for adopting a particular course of action.

business turnaround: Restructuring the business to meet current economic, social, legal, and market trends, and positioning the business and enhancing its products and services to meet consumer demands.

business valuation: The appraisal of the economic value of a business.

consignment (goods on consignment): Goods paid for by retailer only after they have been sold. Unsold goods must be returned to the supplier.

contribution margin: Business Income or revenue minus variable costs.

controllable items: Refers to a cost, revenue, or investment items over which a manager has sufficient influence.

corporation: A form of business ownership. It is treated separately from its owners. It can sue or be sued, engage in contracts, and acquire property. It is owned by shareholders, who enjoy the privilege of limited liability.

cost-benefit: A criterion for choosing among alternative systems whereby the benefits should exceed its expected output at a given cost level.

cost of capital: The cost of alternative sources of financing to the firm if it does not want to use its own money to finance plant, equipment, vehicles, or inventory.

cost center: A responsibility center where the manager can influence costs and is held accountable for a specified output at a given cost.

cost of goods sold: The cost that is associated with units sold during a specific period.

cost of ordering: The cost component in the inventory decision model that represents the amount the company would have to pay to acquire new inventory.

credit characteristics (the five Cs of credit): They are character, capital, capacity, conditions, and collateral. They are used by lenders to determine whether a loan will be repaid on time.

creditor committee: A committee that is set up to operate a company or partnership until an out-of-court settlement is reached.

credit terms: The payment agreement that is part of a credit arrangement. An example would be a 2/10, net 30 arrangement. The customer may deduct 2 percent from the invoice price if s/he pays the invoice within ten days. The full amount of the invoice price is due after ten days, and the customer has thirty days to pay the full amount.

debt utilization ratio: A group of ratios that indicates the extent debt is being used and the prudence with which it is being managed. Calculations include debt to total assets, multiplied by interest earned and fixed charge coverage.

defensible business valuation report: The report/valuation complies with legal and professional standards.

depreciation: The allocation of the initial cost of an asset over its useful life. This amount is deducted from the gross income of the business.

discounted cash flow: A method of valuing expected future cash receipts/revenue and disbursements as of the same date.

dumping: The practice of exporting a product to a foreign country and selling it for less than the price in the domestic market in the home country that produces it; or the practice of selling a product in a foreign country for less than the cost of producing the product in a domestic country. In price-to-price dumping, the exporter uses higher home prices to supplement the reduced revenue from lower export prices. In price-cost dumping, the exporter is subsidized by the local government with duty drawbacks, cash incentives, etc. Dumping is legal under GATT (now the World Trade Organization) rules unless it has an injurious effect that the importing country's producers can establish. If injury is established, GATT rules allow imposition of an antidumping duty that is equal to the difference between the exporter's home-market price and the importer's FOB price.

earnings per share: The earnings that are available to common stockholders divided by the number of common stock shares outstanding.

elective expensing: Writing off the cost of an asset for tax purposes in the year it was purchased, instead of depreciating it over its useful life.

exchange rate: The relationship between the value of two or more currencies. For example, the exchange rate between US dollars and the French franc is stated in dollars per franc or francs per dollar.

factoring: Selling customers' debts (accounts receivables) to a finance company or bank at a discount.

field warehousing: An inventory financing arrangement whereby inventory that is used as collateral (collateralized inventory) is stored on the premises of the borrower but is controlled by an independent warehousing company.

FIFO inventory (First-In-First-Out): Writing off inventory into cost of goods sold, in which the items that were purchased first are used and written off first.

financial risk: The risk that is related to the inability of a company to meet its debt obligations as they come due or reach maturity.

financial statement: A document that shows the income, expenses, assets, and liabilities of a business.

fiscal policy: Government tax policies and the spending that is associated with its tax revenue.

fixed expenses: Expenses that a business must pay monthly, such as rent and utilities.

fixed costs: Costs that are not affected by changes in volume of output. Costs that remain relatively constant regardless of the volume of operations. Example of fixed costs are: rent, straight-line depreciation, property tax, and executive salaries.

float: The difference between the corporation's recorded cash balance on the books and the amount that was credited to its account by the bank.

gross margin: The excess of sales over the cost of goods sold.

hedging (hedging your bets): Engaging in a transaction that partially or fully reduces a prior risk exposure by taking a position that is the opposite to your initial position.

income method of valuation: This is one of several methods used to value a business. It is based on what the business can be expected to earn. This is how buyers will analyze your company to determine what they can expect to earn (in cash) from it.

international taxation: A specialized area of discipline in taxation. It is the study and practical application of a myriad of territorial tax laws and tax treaties that relates to individuals, businesses, and government agencies conducting cross-border trading and overseas commerce.

installment loan: A borrowing arrangement in which a series of equal weekly, biweekly, or monthly payments are used to pay off a loan.

investment tax credit: A credit that you can use to reduce your business tax. It is an incentive for investing in depreciable tangible property.

learning curve: How long it would take a new worker to learn the job.

liabilities: The value of everything that a business or person owes creditors (loans, taxes, mortgages, etc.).

liquidation: The sale of assets to pay creditors (machinery, equipment, vehicles, inventory, etc.). A procedure that may be carried out under bankruptcy law when reorganization of a company does not appear to be feasible, and it appears that the assets of the company are worth more in liquidation than through reorganization.

liquidity: The relative ease of converting short-term assets (bonds, stocks, etc.) to cash.

managerial/management accounting: A method of accounting that is primarily concerned about how accounting can serve internal decision makers.

margin of safety: The excess of actual or budgeted sales over break-even sales.

market method (market approach) of valuation: It is one of several methods used to value a business. This valuation approach is motivated by the quality and quantity of relevant data that is available. Appraisers will look at comparable companies, market rates of return, and the risk factors that are specific to your business to determine the multiples.

net operating loss (NOL): The excess of a taxpayer's (business's or individual's) deductions over gross income in a particular year.

net operating loss deduction: The amount of loss that a business or individual can deduct in a carryback or carryforward year.

off-balance sheet (OBS): Not revealing the true value of a company on the balance sheet; omitting an asset or liability or financing activity from a company's balance sheet.

operational audit: A comprehensive examination and appraisal of an entity's operations to assure management that operations are performed in a manner that complies with established policies and objectives.

payback period: A technique used when considering the purchase of business equipment and other capital expenditures—how many years it would take to recover the initial net investment in an asset.

performance audit: An audit that provides an independent view about whether management and other personnel are efficient and effective in carrying out their responsibilities.

production budget: A detailed plan showing the number of units that must be produced during a period to meet sales and inventory needs.

profit center: A responsibility center where the manager can influence both revenues and expenses for the center.

realistic price expectation: A price that a willing seller and a willing buyer will agree to in an arms-length transaction, each party having the same set of facts. A transaction that a court will approve after looking at the same set of facts.

relevant market data: Information that relates to your market or industry.

R&D tax credit: A tax credit for money spent on research and development.

responsible party: Persons who are responsibility for making assertions in financial prospective statements.

revolving line of credit: A loan attached to a business or personal checking account. It replenishes itself whenever the borrower uses it and pays it back.

sales: The income or revenue generated by the business.

sensitivity analysis: An assessment of the effects of risk or uncertainty on the cash flow of a business.

socioeconomic: The social status and economic condition of a country or people.

sociopolitical: The social status of a country or people and the political nature or climate in that country.

special report: A report requiring specific reporting procedures, such as (1) audits of financial statements prepared in accordance with a basis of accounting other than GAAP, (2) audits of specific accounts or items on financial statements, (3) reports on compliance with respect to contractual regulatory requirements, and (4) financial information presented in prescribed forms or schedules.

state of the art: Modern, up to date.

tax avoidance: A strategy such as tax planning, financial planning, or estate planning that a taxpayer uses to legally minimize taxes or legally defer payment of taxes.

tax evasion: An illegal scheme used by a taxpayer to reduce taxes or defer payment of taxes.

transfer pricing: The value placed upon goods or services that are transferred between profit centers of a decentralized company.

transparency: Open to public scrutiny; easy to detect; easy to understand.

valuation method: The method used to appraise/value your business or personal belongings.

variable costing: This is direct costing. It is a form of product costing that charges fixed factory overhead as incurred against the sales/revenue of the period.

working capital: Working capital is a financial metric that represents the operating liquidity that is available to a business entity. A company can be endowed with assets and profitability but be short of liquidity if its assets cannot readily be converted into cash. Positive working capital is required to ensure that a company has sufficient funds to continue its daily operations and satisfy its maturing short-term debt and upcoming operational expenses. The management of working capital involves managing:

1. Product or merchandise inventories
2. Accounts receivable or customers' debts to your company
3. Accounts payable or creditors your company owes
4. Money in the petty cash account, money in the bank account, and money in the savings account

RESOURCES

(You may read my book, or you may read the thirty-four books below.)

- *The Business of Me*
  Your Job, Your Career, Your Value
  By Linwood Bailey

- *The Ten Roads to Riches*
  The Ways the Wealthy Got There and How You Can Too
  By Ken Fisher with Lara Hoffman

- *The Enlightened Entrepreneur*
  Making an Impact and an Income Doing
  What You Love

- By Olivia Lobell

- *Getting a Job in Hedge Funds*
  An Inside Look at How Funds Hire

- By Adam Zoia with Aaron Finkel

- *Financing Start-Ups*
  How to Raise Money for Emerging Companies
  By Brown and Gutterman

- *The Complete Guide to Buying a Business*
  By Richard Snowden

- *The Denny's Story*
  How a Company in Crisis Resurrected Its Good Name
  By Jim Adamson

- *Taking Charge*
  Management Guide to Troubled Companies and Turnarounds
  By John Whitney

- *Start and Run a Money-Making Bar*
  By Bruce Fier

- *The End of Business as Usual*
  Beware the Way You Work to Succeed in the Consumer Revolution
  By Brian Solis

- *Dealers, Healers, Brutes and Saviors*
  Eight Winning Styles for Solving Giant Business Crisis
  By Gerald and Susan Meyers

- *How to Run a Thriving Business*
  Strategies for Success and Satisfaction

- By Ralph Warner

- *The Accidental Billionaires*
  By Ben Mezrich

- *Venture Capital Handbook*
  An Entrepreneur's Guide to Raising Venture Capital
  By David and Laura Gladstone

- *The Ernst & Young Guide to*
  Financing for Growth
  By Garner, Owen and Conway

- *How to Prepare an*
  Initial Public Offering
  By Riley and Simons

- *Marketing Management*
  Analysis, Planning, Implementing and Control
  By Philip Kotler

- *Professional's Guide to Value Pricing*
  By Ronald Baker

- *Corporate Valuation*
  Tools for Effective Appraisal and Decision Making
  By Bradford Cornell

- *The Market Approach to Valuing Businesses*
  By Shannon Pratt

- *The Money Class*
  Learning to Create Your New American Dream
  By Suze Orman

- *All about Hedge Funds*
  The Easy Way to Get Started
  By Robert Jaeger

- *The Tax Guide for Traders*
  By Robert Green

- *Business and Society*
  Ethics and Stakeholder Management
  By Archie Carroll and Ann Buchholtz

- *Managing Human Resources*
  By Sherman, Bohlander, and Snell

- *Marketing Myths That Are Killing Business*
  The Cure for Death Wish Marketing
  By Kevin Clancy and Robert Shulman

- *Essentials of Managerial Finance*
  By J. Fred Weston, Scott Besley,
  and Eugene Brigham

- *Forensic and Investigative Accounting*
  By Crumbley, Heitger, and Smith

- *Fraud*
  Bringing Light to the Dark Side of Business
  By Albrecht, Wernz, and Williams

- *Lean Accounting*
  Best Practices for Sustainable Integration
  By Joe Stenzel

- *Breaking into the Trade Game*
  A Small Business Guide to Exporting
  By Diane Publishing

- *Exporting from Start to Finance*
  A Comprehensive Guide
  By L. Fargo Wells and Karin Dulat

- *IRS Tax Collection Procedures*
  A Manual for Practitioners
  By Robert Schriebman

- *Battling the IRS*
  Taxpayers Guide to Responding to IRS Notices and Assessments
  By David Silverman